EXPERIENCING GOD'S LOVE IN THE

Deep, Soulful Places

by Elizabeth J Pierce

Experiencing God's Love in the

Deep
Soulful
Places

Elizabeth J. Pierce

CASTLE QUAY BOOKS

Experiencing God's Love in the Deep, Soulful Places

Copyright ©2014 Elizabeth Pierce

All rights reserved
Printed in Canada
International Standard Book Number 978-1-927355-58-9
ISBN 978-1-927355-59-6 EPUB

Published by:
Castle Quay Books
Pickering, Ontario
Tel: (416) 573-3249
E-mail: info@castlequaybooks.com   www.castlequaybooks.com

Edited by Marina Hofman Willard, and Lori MacKay
Cover design by Burst Impressions
Printed at Essence Printing, Belleville, Ontario

Scripture quotations, unless otherwise indicated, are from *The Holy Bible, New International Version*. Copyright © 1973, 1978, 1984, 2011 by International Bible Society. Used by permission of Zondervan Publishing House.

• Scripture quotations marked NASB are taken from the New American Standard Bible ®. Copyright © 1960, 1962, 1963, 1968, 1971, 1972, 1973, 1975, 1977, 1995 by THE LOCKMAN FOUNDATION. All rights reserved. Scripture quotations marked KJV are from *The Holy Bible, King James Version*. Copyright © 1977, 1984, Thomas Nelson Inc., Publishers. All rights reserved. Scripture quotations marked NKJV are taken from the New King James Version. Copyright © 1979, 1980, 1982. Thomas Nelson Inc., Publishers. Scriptures marked ESV are taken from *The Holy Bible*, English Standard Version. © 2001 by Crossway Bibles, a division of Good News Publishers. All rights reserved. Scripture quotations marked (NLT) are taken from the Holy Bible, New Living Translation, copyright © 1996, 2004, 2007, 2013 by Tyndale House Foundation. Used by permission of Tyndale House Publishers, Inc., Carol Stream, Illinois 60188. All rights reserved. Scripture quotations marked AMP are taken from *The Amplified Bible*, Old Testament, copyright © 1965, 1987 by the Zondervan Corporation. *The Amplified New Testament*, copyright © 1954, 1958, 1987 by the Lockman Foundation. Used by permission. Scripture quotations marked ISV are from The Holy Bible: International Standard Version® Release 2.1, Copyright © 1996-2012 The ISV Foundation, ALL RIGHTS RESERVED INTER-NATIONALLY.

Library and Archives Canada Cataloguing in Publication

Pierce, Elizabeth, 1972-, author
    Experiencing God's love in the deep, soulful places /
Elizabeth Pierce.

Issued in print and electronic formats.
ISBN 978-1-927355-58-9 (pbk.).—ISBN 978-1-927355-59-6
(epub)

    1. God (Christianity)—Love. I. Title.

BT140.P54 2014   231'.6
C2014-906372-5

    C2014-906373-3

CASTLE QUAY BOOKS

Table of Contents

This book is from Him, and for Him

Author's Note

I was three and a half when he died. I don't remember him at all, and I don't remember anything about the morning he died, although I was right there. I have likely repressed the memory, and I may never remember it now, since almost four decades have passed.

People tell me I was the apple of his eye. That he called me "Precious." They tell me he was fiercely protective of me, and that he doted on me. I like to hear how my dad was with me, but I don't remember any of it.

Funny thing is, I know I knew him. I feel it. It's the pain bursting in my chest when I watch a movie or read a book about a child whose parent dies. It's not empathy I feel. It's my own loss. I know it in every fibre of my being. There's no picture story in my head to recall...no events that flash in my mind...no smells or sounds to help me piece together the events. No memory of it at all, but I *know* I was loved. When I hear those stories about him, deep within me there is agreement. Some part of me remembers and says, "Yes, that is exactly how it was." We were strongly connected.

Before I wrote this book, I had been exploring with God more of what it means, personally and intimately, to be loved by Him. As I stepped back, I could see how my entire life has been full of experiences that make up one unending love letter from Him to me. What God has shown me is that understanding His love is a lot like my experience of knowing I was loved by my dad. It's not really something you can make sense of in your head. It's something you have to feel and experience deep within you—at the core of who He made you.

You have your own unending love letter from Him.

Like me, you are called by God to make a difference. In my various roles as a therapist, speaker and leader, God has laid on my heart to share what truly makes a difference in a life: His love for us. This book is my attempt to show what grasping the reality of that unending love really means in the deep places where our hurts, our woundedness and the realities of our imperfect lives are hidden and often collide with His vision for our future.

Knowing the reality of His love goes deeper than anything else can, filling the crevices of our souls when we embrace the fullness of it.

I pray that you will be blessed by this book and that you will hear His heart in my words, the heart of the Author of the ultimate love story written just for you.

In Him,

Elizabeth

CHAPTER ONE

What's So Amazing About Love?

*Three things will last forever—faith, hope, and love—
and the greatest of these is love.*

1 Corinthians 13:13 (NLT)

What's so amazing about love? *Everything.*

Isn't that why our entertainment industry is saturated by romance? Isn't that why soap operas are still alive and well today, even though the plots get more convoluted every year? It was reported that over 8 million viewers tuned in to watch the 2012 season's finale of *The Bachelorette*—why? Because humans love a good love story, and most people want to believe in the fairy-tale ending of "happily ever after" and finding one's true love.

Love is wonderful! It is better than the perfect summer day; more refreshing than a cold glass of water when you are hot; more soothing than a massage; more beautiful than the most famous painting; more exciting than the best amusement park ride; more motivating than the best personal trainer; and more inspiring than the latest motivational speaker. Love is so vital for every single human being that ultimately the desire to love and be loved supersedes most other earthly human pursuits.

As women, the desire to *feel* loved often trumps other relationship needs. To feel loved. Cherished. Special. Worth something. These feelings are so important to us that they feel almost as necessary to our ability to thrive as air, food and water.

We crave love. We seek it out. We celebrate it when it happens and grieve it when it is gone. But what we are wired for is more than just a wonderful romance. And it is more secure than the love of a best friend. *True* love (I can't say those two words together without thinking of the movie *The Princess Bride*) is about so much more. The kind of love we crave deep down in the depths of our being is life-changing. It's the answer we are all searching for.

Deep, Soulful Places

The Need We All Have—Whether We Admit It or Not

I clearly remember the conversation with my mom. I was only four and a half, but for some reason I remember. She was tucking me into bed one night after we had been out for a celebration dinner with family and friends. We were celebrating her engagement to Mr. Gee. Mr. Gee was a quiet, gentle man. He was also a widower, his wife having died of cancer when his daughter was six and his son was three. I liked Mr. Gee a lot. He made my mom happy, and I was told that when he married my mom, he would become my dad. Did I ever like that idea! I really, really wanted a dad again. I missed mine so much. I would often ask my mom if we could talk to Jesus so I could "ask Jesus to tell Daddy that I love him and miss him." And God bless my mom, she always did, even though I suspect it tore viciously at her open wound. I didn't think about that at the time. I only thought about the hole in my own heart that used to be filled with my dad's love and attention—and I wanted it full again.

A new daddy sounded like the perfect answer. But I didn't want to have to call my new dad *Mr. Gee*. So, as my mom was tucking me in, I said, "Mommy, do you think that Mr. Gee would mind if I called him Daddy after you get married?"

My mom stroked my face and smiled through tears. "I think that would be fine with Mr. Gee, dear."

I didn't realize it at the time, but what I was longing for was love. A father's love. And in my little-girl world, I was hoping that by calling Mr. Gee *Daddy* he would be that loving father figure I had lost and somehow instinctively knew I needed back again. Thank God, he was.

After almost two decades of providing therapy, I have had many opportunities to observe humans and their reactions to their sometimes horrendous life experiences. And there has always been one common denominator: those who have been loved at some point in their lives fare far better than those who have never felt loved.

In the early 1900s psychiatrist John Bowlby came out with his now renowned attachment theory, which in essence purports that early attachment of an infant to a primary caregiver forms the basis from which that child comes to understand and relate to the world. It suggests there are three basic needs that must be met: safety, security and belonging (significance). As infants and children have those needs repeatedly met (or not) over time, they come to form their understanding of themselves, relationships and the world around them. However, there are many individuals who have not always had positive early development experiences, but if they have felt deeply loved by someone at some point in their lives, it sustains them and offers them some resiliency and motivation to cope and carry on, despite their pain, trauma or woundedness. In fact, it would seem that this need to be loved is so deeply ingrained that most of our human behaviour is influenced by it, either directly or indirectly.

As a therapist, I have noticed that love is one of the reasons many women stay in abusive relationships, elderly parents tolerate abuse by their offspring, and children blame themselves for their abuse instead of their abusive parent. It makes movie stars jump on couches on national television. It makes people leave their lives and start fresh somewhere else with that special someone. It makes a little girl want to call the nice man in her mom's life "Daddy." It is a powerful emotion that we all long for, if we are honest with ourselves. But rarely do we feel completely fulfilled on a human level, despite the most perfect of circumstances.

This is by divine design. Because God ultimately intended it to be *Him* who meets our unquenchable longings for love, safety, security and significance—in those deep, soulful places.

When some of you read that, it may cause you to think that God is cruel—He creates us and then leaves us spinning our wheels and feeling unfulfilled unless we choose to have Him in our lives. Or it may sound like He is manipulative or punitive, orchestrating our lives so that unless we choose to be in a relationship with Him, we'll never get our basic, fundamental needs fully met.

I actually think it is the exact opposite.

I have had many occasions to witness humans who are *not* in a relationship with God go through some very difficult situations, seek therapy, and report feeling better, able to cope, and (from their perspective) "healed" from their experience. *Without Him.* And every time I see this, I am reminded of what a loving, gracious God I serve. Because He created us with a spot that can only be filled by Him, and He desires that we live in relationship with Him. He extends Himself to us, *the* answer to all that we need, and then when we choose to *not* accept Him into the minutia of our lives, we still heal. He "lets" us survive and cope without Him. And *many* people do. That is not punitive or manipulative. That is gracious and loving.

He doesn't react to our rejection in a negative or humanly typical way. He doesn't pick up all His toys and storm home when we say we don't want to play. He doesn't sabotage our party just because He wasn't invited. He doesn't decide "Well, if you won't let Me in to be a part of your healing, I will plague you with nightmares forever and make it so you *never* heal." *That* would be punitive and manipulative, and that is not who He is.

Deep, Soulful Places

It must be so hard on His heart, given how much He loves us, to step aside and accept that we are not inviting Him into our world...into our healing. Because He knows. He knows that the healing, freedom and fulfillment we get when we do life *with* Him is way better than words can express. Because things are as they were designed to be from the beginning of time.

His Love Is Safe and Secure

I had lunch with a long-time friend earlier this week, after having not seen her for months. Wonderfully, we picked up where we left off as though only days had passed. I love that, and I love that our relationship is typified by deep, meaningful connection. We've never had a superficial conversation in the entire time I have known her, 14 years and counting. We just get right down to what's going on in our lives—the good, the bad and the ugly. I know only a handful of people like that, and I consider them gifts from God. Evidence of His love for me.

To have someone like that in my life causes me to reflect on what is at the root of relationships like this. Most of all, I believe it's that I feel safe with her. I know she won't judge me—in fact, even when presented with my failings, she always manages to find some way to encourage me. She never joins in my wallowing. She acknowledges my "warts," but in a way that compels me to think differently and move forward. I could spend the whole time talking about me, and she wouldn't bat an eye. She would make me feel like I was all that mattered. I've never worried about her talking behind my back, and I always know where I stand with her. All of that means I feel secure in my relationship with her. What a gift!

Safety in a relationship is unfortunately often not present. Growing up, I had relationships that were far from emotionally safe for me, where I felt picked on, made fun of, falsely accused or just plain misled. I was often talked about behind my back, and those elementary and early high school years were very painful as a result, although they helped me learn to be discerning about who would be allowed in my "inner circle" as I matured. They taught me what I wanted from the people around me. And at the heart, I needed to be able to answer "yes" to one simple question: Are they safe?

A *secure* relationship is safe—emotionally, physically and spiritually. Safety in relationships becomes the foundation on which you can trust, risk and grow.[1] Because it builds up rather than tears down. It draws you in and makes you want more. It does not make you feel "less than." You can count on the other person to be there for you. There is never a question about where you stand.

---

[1] See John Bowlby, *Attachment and Loss*, 3 vols. (New York: Basic Books, 1969–1980).

That is what God offers us in relationship with Him—the most healthy of relationships. But unlike in human relationships, He is perfect, so He will never let us down. We make mistakes in our relationship with Him, but He will never return the favour. He will never react emotionally in the heat of the moment. Never ignore us. Never forget what matters to us. Never manipulate. Never condemn. Never make us feel responsible for His "issues." Never lead us to believe something other than the truth. Never try to cover up His actions. Never behave selfishly. Never hurt us. Never leave us. Never. You will never have to worry about Him repeating one negative thing that has happened to you in a human relationship. Personalize this for yourself for a minute: whatever unhealthiness you've experienced in human relationships, you can rest assured He won't *ever* do that.

That is safety and security—the way relationships should be. And it is here, for you, with Him. I've often said the only reason I don't have an anxiety disorder is because of my relationship with God and how He meets my needs. My relationship with Him is where I can go with all my worries, fears, confusion, stress and hurt and know with certainty that not only will He not contribute to those feelings, He will also help me cope, at the very least. Because in relationship with God, you can expect perfect love and safety.

That doesn't mean *life* is perfect and safe; it means *He* is perfect and safe, regardless of what is swirling around us. Sometimes we can get deceived into thinking that the promise of His love is some kind of guarantee we can cling to that life will be good or easy, or both. But His promises are about Him and us. Which means that because we live in a fallen world, life may still be hard. That doesn't mean we aren't loved.

I love Isaiah 49:15-16: "*I will not forget you! See, I have engraved you on the palms of my hands.*" My less than emotionally safe experiences with "friends" in my youth made me feel insecure in relationships. Maybe that's why the safety and security of God's love matters so much to me. I know what it feels like to feel emotionally unsafe with someone. I hated the feeling of insecurity that would well up in me as I walked into the classroom to notice a group of girls rolling their eyes at me and hushing each other. (I still occasionally catch myself assuming someone is talking behind my back if I walk into a room and the talking stops.) I hated feeling on the outside looking in, not quite fitting in. Always wondering what others were thinking. It was horrible.

I love the feeling that washes over me when I read that He will never forget me. That feels so safe. I matter. I'm not on the outside with Him. And He has *me*—"Goody-Two-Shoes," "Brainer," eyes-rolled-at, barely-tolerated-by-the-cool-kids me—*engraved* into His palms. Not my name tattooed on His shoulder. Not my picture enclosed in a locket by His heart. No, He has me *engraved* on His hands…the hands He uses to comfort me, to hold me, to steady me, to lead me, to carry me. The hands that were nailed to the cross for me. Yes, I feel I belong, that I'm significant. I feel safe. And I feel more secure than I know how to express in words. Because He loves me. And He loves you that way too.

The Biblical Definition of Love—1 Corinthians 13:1–8, 13

This chapter in the Bible on love is one of the most frequently read chapters at weddings. And it's no surprise that it's so popular. It describes what everyone wants their friend, family and romantic relationships to be like. But it is not only describing earthly love. Read the verses for yourself, and soak in what they are saying about His love for us.

> If I speak in the tongues of men or of angels, but do not have love, I am only a resounding gong or a clanging cymbal. If I have the gift of prophecy and can fathom all mysteries and all knowledge, and if I have a faith that can move mountains, but do not have love, I am nothing. If I give all I possess to the poor and give over my body to hardship that I may boast, but do not have love, I gain nothing.
>
> Love is patient, love is kind. It does not envy, it does not boast, it is not proud. It does not dishonor others, it is not self-seeking, it is not easily angered, it keeps no record of wrongs. Love does not delight in evil but rejoices with the truth. It always protects, always trusts, always hopes, always perseveres. Love never fails…And now these three remain: faith, hope and love. But the greatest of these is love. (1 Corinthians 13:1–8, 13)

How did that feel for you? Could you soak in those words and own them as a description of the love you feel from God? I suspect that some of you can. For me, I picture it feeling like the soothing comfort that a hot bath brings to tired, cold bones (a long, hot bath is my go-to for most of what ails me).

For others, it may have caused a longing in you to soak those words in and own them in your life. You *know* there is a bathtub; you just don't know what it feels like to soak in it and be soothed and comforted by its warmth. For whatever reason, you've only ever taken a shower. Never to soak in the warm water—it's only been to get clean.

I also need to acknowledge that some of you may not have been able to think about that description of love in relation to God and His love for you because of how far it is from your current earthly relationships. They have tainted your view of all love. Many relationships are less than ideal.

For almost two decades I have sat with women as they have grieved the loss of the relationships they thought would offer them this kind of love and have had to work on healing from the abuse they suffered instead. I've also sat with countless women as they have worked through the pain caused by unmet needs and hurt and dysfunction in their families. And I've walked this path with friends and family members as well. So, I know that for some, hearing "I love you" doesn't feel anything like 1 Corinthians 13. It feels a lot more like a maximum security prison. That is not what God wants for you in any relationship. Especially not with Him.

Let's just look one more time at the words that describe love. I've included in parentheses what I believe the "love is" equivalent would be. I like thinking about things in terms of what *is*. Patient. Kind. Doesn't envy (love is happy for others). Doesn't boast (love is modest). Not proud (love is humble). Not rude (love is polite). Not self-seeking (love is selfless). Not easily angered (love is stable). Keeps no record of wrongs (love is forgiving). Does not delight in evil, but rejoices with the truth. Always protects. Always trusts. Always hopes. Always perseveres. Never fails (love is reliable). *Never. God's* love never fails, anyway. Which is why it is the *only* love that will fill that deep longing we all have.

The Greatest of These…

Love is the greatest because without it faith and hope have no place to anchor themselves—like a helium balloon caught in a gust of wind, blown away before it can be tied to the arm of a little child. It's hard to have faith in something without the sustaining power of love as the foundation on which it rests. It's hard to hope without the safety of love to tenderly hold and protect its delicate flower. And it is the greatest because love is at the heart of the most profound act of mercy ever offered to humankind.

Very few people would disagree with the premise that there is no greater sacrifice to offer for another human than life itself. When we honour our fallen and standing heroes and give special recognition to firefighters and police officers, we are honouring people who have chosen a profession that by its very nature puts their lives at risk for the sake of another. We also recognize "everyday heroes"—people who find themselves unintentionally faced with a choice to risk their lives to help someone else, or not. We only get one life, and to be willing to put that stranger and that life ahead of one's own in the moment of crisis is remarkable. They deserve recognition.

Deep, Soulful Places

You hear about the bond that gets created between rescuers and those rescued—this inexplicable connection that results from that life-saving experience. Both parties ending up forever changed, with a greater appreciation for the life they've been given and the inherent value that exists therein. Like I said, very few people would argue with any of this. It's an accepted fact in society today.

Now let's spiritualize this concept. What the Bible says about love is *truth,* so it's the foundation for this discussion. You will likely need to remind yourself of the truth periodically as we move forward from here, because it's in the spiritual application of things that the enemy of our souls tries to rob us of what God means for us to experience about His love.

The verses in the Bible about God's love for us are both numerous and powerful. However, there are a few that really spell out the spiritual application for us (see appendix A for additional verses). *"For God **so** loved the world, that he gave his only Son"* (John 3:16, ESV, emphasis added). *"Greater love has no one than this, that one lay down his life for his friends"* (John 15:13, NASB). *"God showed how much he loved us by sending his one and only Son into the world so that we might have eternal life through him. This is real love—not that we loved God, but that he loved us and sent his Son as a sacrifice to take away our sins"* (1 John 4:9–10, NLT).

God did for you and me what we call heroic today. Jesus' life (the rescuer) was given for us (the rescued). Because He loves us.

I have a friend who has lived through more in her lifetime than most people would think humanly possible to endure. Her trauma experiences are many and go beyond imagination (think ritualistic abuse and all that entails). There has been so much pain and woundedness in her life, it has not been easy for her to understand that she has value because God loves her.

In fact, I would say that until this past year, she did not fully grasp it. She believed in the story of salvation and told many others about it. She memorized Bible verses and immersed herself in the Bible, care groups and serving in the church. She did everything she thought was pleasing to God, but it didn't translate into anything meaningful to her. She thought she was worthless, unlovable. Jesus' love and sacrifice for her had remained trapped in her head—it had not seeped into the fibres of her being. Over the years of her torture, Satan had done a really good job of convincing her that her abuse defined her and was a reflection of her lack of worth. So that's what she felt. Not love. Even though the love was there for her. She had taken a shower to get clean, but she had never soaked in the warm bath of His love.

I know this woman well. And I know why the enemy worked so hard to keep her feeling worthless and unlovable. She will not keep quiet about something she believes in, and he knew if she *felt* the magnitude of God's love, her testimony would be unstoppable. So he tried to silence her by making her feel worthless to the point of death. Literally. She miraculously survived many suicide attempts. The problem was a lack of connection between her head and her heart. She knew in her head that it meant her salvation, and she was grateful for it. But as for what that sacrifice meant about her worth and God's love—she just couldn't feel it in those deep, soulful places. As a result, with the enemy's lies about her deep wounds clawing at her, her life was precarious. She never knew when she would be spiralling down into the depths of despair again, ultimately ending in an attempt to take her own life.

One day (it still brings tears to my eyes), I got the most amazing email from her. She wrote to tell me this:

> I feel prompted to tell you what I have just settled with the Lord. I am chosen and dearly loved. I was bought at a high price. Value and worth are determined by the price paid for them. Therefore I have great value. I am worthy because Jesus bought me for the value He sees in me. This is a message I am to bring to the people of God. A message I am to spread to the world. We are chosen and dearly loved.

Those deep, soulful parts were finally filled. The scales were finally off her eyes, and she could see. She has great value. Why? Because Jesus loves her, so much that He died for her. And if He was willing to give His life for her, then she has value. It's that simple and yet that powerful. So she no longer tries to end her own life, because she realizes she is worth something. Nothing else changed in her life except for her understanding of what it means to be loved. Loved so much she was worth dying for. God's love for her had moved from the place it held in her head, as a theological concept and truth, down into her soul to become something that was personally hers.

It's like when you decorate a bedroom, and you have every item you need to make it complete—except for the lamp to go on your nightstand. You have found one, but it costs way more than you can afford. So you put it on layaway, pay your down payment and establish your payment plan. The lamp is technically yours once you have paid it off in full. But it isn't in your home yet, so it doesn't really *feel* like you own it. When you walk into the bedroom and scan the room, you try to picture the light on the nightstand, but because it's just a picture in your head, it's not the same. All you see is the empty spot where the light belongs, and it makes you long for it all the more.

And then comes the day when you make your final payment. It changes everything to see the light sitting in that once empty space, completing the room. It's been yours since payment began, but now it feels like you own it because it's where it belongs…where it was intended to be all along.

What's so amazing about love? It is life-changing—life-saving. Remember 1 Corinthians 13:13? *"Three things will last forever—faith, hope, and love—and the greatest of these is love"* (NLT). My friend had faith. She kept hoping things would feel better. But things got better because of love, the greatest of the three. Ultimately, love is the greatest because God *is* love (1 John 4:16). It is a description of Him.

Reflect for a moment on your own life experiences or those of someone you know well. Can you think of a personal application that points to why faith and hope are important and valuable but love trumps them both? Maybe your experience isn't as drastic as my friend's. Maybe you haven't been brought back from the brink of suicide because Jesus loves you. Or maybe you have. It's far more common than most people believe. Because so many of us, even strong, seasoned believers, don't truly grasp why love is the greatest…what it really means for our lives.

A Children's Song Sums It Up

Lately I've been thinking that what is most important about the Christian faith is perfectly summed up in the first line of a popular children's Sunday school song: "Jesus loves me, this I know, for the Bible tells me so."

There are so many different denominations. So many different interpretations of the Bible. But really, when you sort through and pull out what really matters, what ultimately makes a difference in someone's life is this: Jesus loves us. Everything else flows from that one basic truth.

It was *because* of His love that He went to the cross to die for us. The love was there first. It was *because* of His love that He did things differently than the religious leaders who were out for their own glory. It was *because* of His love that He healed people. It was *because* of His love that He performed miracles. Everything good, right and true was and is *because* of His love. Everything. The whole Old Testament is about how God orchestrated and set in motion world events leading up to Christ's death on the cross. *Because* of His love. Genesis 1:1 (*"In the beginning God created"*) happened *because* of God's love.

Imagine that for a moment. Unlock the part of you that used to dress up, play school or imagine fantasy worlds—whatever you did with your imagination that caused you joy. Picture being the heroine of a land where everything miraculous, beautiful and good is because of how loved *you* are. What do you feel about that? Now consider—this is not a figment of your imagination. This is real life, with God.

It's not surprising that a children's song captures the *truth*. Jesus said in Matthew 18:3 that unless you become like a child you will not enter the kingdom of heaven. God has always placed great value on a child's simple way of looking at Him…stripped of all the trappings of our complicated adult minds, back to the simple, powerful, bottom-line truth: Jesus loves me, this I *know*, for the Bible tells me so.

I can almost hear some of the backlash to what I have just said. Please don't misunderstand. I'm not discounting the many other very important truths that are found in the Bible. I'm just saying that when push comes to shove, when you are talking someone back from the edge of a cliff (figuratively or literally), you need to be able to be concise, powerful and convincing. It may be your only chance. So what sums it up? What matters most? Some would say salvation, through Jesus's death and resurrection. That is true, but what prompted that? Yes, our sin made it necessary for there to be a sacrifice, I know. But what prompted that *particular* sacrifice? His love for us.

Remember one of the verses I quoted earlier? Pay attention to the way it is worded: "*For God **so** loved the world that he gave his one and only Son*" (John 3:16, emphasis added). He *so* loved the world. It doesn't say, "For God detested our sin, so He sent His one and only Son." It doesn't say, "God knew He was the only way to fix man's sin, so He sent His only Son." It doesn't say, "For God loved the world, He gave His one and only Son." It says, "For God *so* loved the world." This verse means that God loved the world in a manner that caused Him to send His only Son to die. That's a pretty powerful, strong kind of love to compel that kind of sacrifice, don't you think? God loved us so much that He demonstrated His great love for us by sending His only Son to die.

But what does that mean? How does being the object of that kind of passionate love move you? You are *so* loved. Do you *feel so* loved? You may be able to answer these questions with a firm and sure answer. And that is amazing if you can. But if you can't, please don't lose heart. And know you are not alone…*getting to the answers to those questions is the very reason we began this journey together.*

At times, what His love feels like doesn't fit in a neat and tidy churchy box. (It is worth noting that at this stage in the journey for some, it may not feel neat and tidy at all…it may feel disappointing, confusing and painful.) And that's okay. We will walk this road together—there is hope.

Since we just talked about God's view of children, I thought I'd ask my children how it feels and what being *so* loved by God means to them. I've decided to share with you what they came up with, because I think it shows how God reaches in and reveals His love to us in ways that meet us where we are.

Here are a few examples of what my boys, Caleb, 8, and Ethan, 11, said: "It feels like always meeting new friends" (my extreme extrovert); "It reminds me of getting a new present, like a puppy. You feel so happy" (Caleb's desperate for a dog); "It feels like winning the Stanley Cup over and over again" (Ethan loves hockey); "It's like giving someone a hug after a long day."

Take a minute now and make your own list. I've started mine. So far I have: a soothing warm bath for cold, tired bones; finally bringing home the missing piece to complete my room; safe and secure. Perhaps you could find a journal to use throughout your reading of this book, as I will often suggest that you do some writing and reflecting as we go on (sorry, it's the therapist in me). It will likely be helpful to assess your list. Add to it as He reveals Himself to you. Correct it as He opens your eyes to His *truth.* Put tick marks beside places where you have it totally right. Because He wants you to know how it *feels* and what it *means* to be loved by Him.

I invite you to join me as I explore the depth and breadth of God's love and how this safe, secure, worth-giving, life-changing, sacrifice-compelling love impacts the most precious, sacred parts of our being. My prayer is that as we take this journey together, you will be able to see past my thoughts and words to the One who loves you and to what He has planned for you in relationship with Him.

CHAPTER TWO

Love Means No Condemnation

*For God did not send his son into the world to condemn
the world, but to save the world through Him.*

John 3:16

Those of you who consider yourselves seasoned believers may feel like this chapter has little relevance. Like sitting through a gospel message. I would consider myself a pretty seasoned believer, and it has great relevance for me.

Not too long ago I did something to my husband, Todd, that I felt was wrong, and I was beside myself about it. I shared something with a friend of ours, for prayer, that involved my husband. Not something bad about him, just something that was part of our journey. These are friends we "do life" with. They know us and all our "stuff." This is what we talk about with them, and this level of authenticity characterizes our relationship. Yet, after I shared with her, I felt regret. I wished I hadn't done so—I wished I had checked with Todd first before I opened my big mouth, because it was really his story, not mine, to share. I felt sick about it.

By the time the end of the day had come and I had time alone with Todd to talk about it, I had built it up in my head to be a major breech in trust that I had committed against him, and I feared he would feel very betrayed by me and that it would affect his ability to feel emotionally safe with me going forward. I was beating myself up pretty badly about it all—first because he is the last person on earth I would ever want to cause any upset to, and second because I am a therapist. Confidentiality is what I do for a living. I should know better.

After we got the kids into bed, I sat down beside my husband (ready to vomit) and told him that I had done something very wrong that I needed to confess to him. The poor guy got a really concerned look on his face, turned off the TV and faced me. I then proceeded to tell him what I had shared with our friend and that I felt it was very wrong—that it was his story to share, and I should have talked with him about sharing it before I just did so.

His concerned look completely disappeared and was replaced with an expression of relief. Then he furrowed his brow, shook his head and said, "Babe, that is not a big deal at all. Don't worry about it! I totally trust [our friend], and I am completely fine with you telling her so they can pray."

I couldn't believe how *huge* of a deal I had made it in my head and how little of a deal it was in reality to my husband. It was such a reminder to me of just how powerful condemnation can be. It can take a non-issue and make it into a monster issue. It can twist a normal situation and make it into an immobilizing one. It can move you from good to bad in your head in a split second if you are not careful. It can make you think you have damaged your marital intimacy by seeking the prayer support of those who love you, when in fact you haven't.

Condemnation caused me to think that my husband's trust in me, love for me and emotional safety with me might be compromised. And more than that, truth be told, condemnation had me feeling like I didn't even deserve any of that from him. All because of something *I* thought was a mistake.

Condemnation does that to us with God too. It gets us thinking we aren't good enough. That He couldn't love us or want us around after what we have or have not done. And God responds like my husband. "I love you. It's not a big deal to Me, because I covered that already with Jesus and the cross."

Why did I say that being so loved by God means no condemnation, instead of saying that it means salvation? (I believe that the only way we are actually free from condemnation is because of salvation through Christ Jesus—please see appendix E if you would like to read my thoughts about this a bit more.) Because I believe it is much easier for women to accept the idea of salvation than the idea of no condemnation. Think back to the story I shared earlier about my friend if you need a real-life illustration of what I mean. If we feel condemned, even though we are saved, we certainly won't feel so loved. Or valuable. Or worth much.

The Daughter of Love: Grace

I love grace. It's what I was met with in the eyes of my husband when I sat down beside him, before he even knew what I was going to tell him. He tells me it is because of how much he loves me—he hates to see me upset, even when he is the one who has been wronged. It's in those moments that I find myself keenly aware of the verses that talk about Christ as the bridegroom and the Church as the bride. This is how He responds to us. He loves us *so* much despite all the things we have done wrong that when He looks at us, He is moved by His love and doesn't condemn us. He offers us grace.

Why do I make mention of grace when we are supposed to be talking about love? Grace is because of love. It's an outgrowth of love. It's almost an action word for love. And it's what we are met with instead of condemnation. When I was a teenager, I heard a preacher at Joy Bible Camp say, "Grace is God's hand giving us what we don't deserve, and mercy is His hand holding back what we do deserve."

Why would God show us mercy and grace?

Because He loves us.

But, because God loves us, He also made us with free will. He doesn't force us to love Him or obey Him; nor does He make us like robots, to follow Him blindly and without choice. Adam and Eve were given a choice, and they didn't listen. They didn't choose God's way. But because God loves us, He doesn't give up on us...*ever.* Adam and Eve sinned and broke the perfect relationship with God, but there is a second chance. We don't have to remain destined to a life without God. Jesus Christ died on the cross and rose again to take care of the price that needed to be paid. That sacrifice was made for us, out of love.

And because of that love, God lavishes us with grace. Psalm 103:12 says that as far as the east is from the west, that's how far our sins are removed from us because of Him. That is grace He shows us because we are *so* loved. That is Him holding back what we deserve...so far back that it's as far away as the east is from the west. So that we are not "just" saved; we are free from condemnation. Because our sins are removed from us through Jesus, we don't have to worry about being condemned. It's all been taken care of. Romans 8:1 says, "*Therefore, there is now* **no** *condemnation for those who are in Christ Jesus*" (emphasis added). Because we believe, we are no longer condemned. Now, or for eternity.

Funny how the Bible can say that so clearly, yet we can be so fuzzy about what it means. It doesn't say that if you should have known better you will be condemned. It doesn't say that you may be condemned if it was one of the "big" sins. It doesn't say that if you keep doing the same thing wrong you will be condemned. It doesn't say that you really should be perfect because you are to be like Christ, so you will be condemned. It doesn't say that if you were abused there's something wrong with you, so you are condemned. It doesn't say that although you are forgiven you should continue to beat yourself up for past mistakes so that you won't be condemned. It says there is *no* condemnation. *None.* He *so* loves us, and there is *no* condemnation in Him. Those two things are a big deal! Most of us can think of at least one relationship we've had at some point in our lives where we felt there were strings attached. You won the person's favour, but it came at a price to you. You had to do something, go somewhere, act in some way to please the other person. Everything was dependent on you and how you behaved, and if you measured up, it all worked out. I sure had my share of those relationships when I was younger.

In fact, much of life feels like this, doesn't it? We feel we are always trying to measure up to something or someone—whether it be a societal standard for physical appearance, professional performance, relationship status or some kind of achievement. And when we think we haven't measured up—or worse, when we are *told* we don't measure up—that is such a horrible feeling. We feel terrible about ourselves. We feel condemned.

There is none of that when we are being *so* loved by God. We are already good enough in His eyes. (Hold your theological reactions here, please—I'm not saying good enough to enter heaven; I'm saying good enough to be loved. He loved us before we loved Him, remember?) And it is safe with Him. There's no criticism. No more "less than." No more "not as good as." No more making amends. No walking on eggshells. No bending over backwards to please. It's done. It's taken care of. *Jesus* took care of it all when He died for you and for me. And because He did that, He made it so that once we accept this awesome love offering, we can sit back and bask in the amazing mystery of being *so* loved by His Father.

We don't often do that, though, do we? Sit back and bask in His love? Spend time just reflecting on how much He loves us and how secure that love will always be—either through alone time with Him, in His Word, listening to praise music or reading something that draws our hearts and minds to that place. I would dare to suggest that it doesn't happen nearly as frequently or with as many people as it could, for a few reasons.

One reason may be that there is yet to be a relationship established. Perhaps there has not yet been an acceptance of being *so* loved by Him, so there has never been a sense of needing or wanting to bask in the love. The person is still in the searching phase. Or they don't yet realize what is there waiting for them...the extent to which they are loved. I also think it is because many people are like I used to be before I began this journey with God. They believe with their whole hearts, and they understand (in their heads) the theological teachings of the Christian Church about being loved by God. But their head knowledge has never translated into the action of sitting back and just soaking up His love.

Another reason I don't think it happens often enough with enough people is because we are not used to this kind of love. Add the fact that we are such a busy society. We do not do very well at taking time for things, let alone basking in something! We are used to doing something. Used to action. Most of us struggle to sit in a chair by the water for 20 minutes reading a book (which is still technically doing something!), let alone sitting back and basking in God's love.

Forgiveness

An even more common reason people don't sit and bask in His love, in my personal and professional experience, is the issue of not forgiving ourselves. We are not condemned in Christ. But we are condemned in self. I can be horrible at forgiving myself when I make mistakes. Especially if they are mistakes that negatively impact another person, like hurting someone I love. I have walked around for years beating myself up for things I have done wrong that I feel I shouldn't have. I've confessed them to God (if you are not clear about why you do this even though you are already saved, I've shared my thoughts about this in appendix F), which means I'm forgiven, but I don't feel forgiven. Why? Because of myself! Well, I actually think it's because I'm allowing the enemy to deceive me into thinking that my mistake was bad enough or that I should have known better and, therefore, somehow, I'm still kind of "on the hook" for it.

But think about that. Do you know what that really means? If I keep myself (or someone else for that matter) "on the hook" for a wrong that has been done but has been confessed to and forgiven by God, what I am saying in essence is that Jesus' death on the cross wasn't good enough for me. My sin can't be covered by His sacrifice. Which means that I'm saying that those verses like Romans 8:1 aren't *truth*. Which ultimately means that I'm saying that God is a liar. That He didn't really mean He would save us through Jesus' death on the cross. If I'm still on the hook for mistakes that I've made, said sorry for and asked forgiveness for, if I'm condemned for them still, God is a liar.

I don't believe that God is a liar. In fact, I *know* that God is not a liar. He is *truth*. Titus 1:2 says God does not lie. But the Bible does say that Satan is the father of lies, and that there is no truth in him (John 8:44). So, when I find myself feeling something that does not measure up with what the Bible says (the *truth*), then I know it is not the truth. It is a lie. Which means, I know where it comes from. I also have a pretty good clue about where it comes from because of how it affects me.

When we feel condemned, we don't feel all warm and fuzzy. We usually feel really rotten and want to avoid whatever it is that makes us feel that way. I think that is the whole point of self-condemnation. Of feeling guilty. Of being plagued by guilt, guilt-ridden, driven by our guilt. The enemy of our souls wants to make us feel so rotten about our relationship with God that we pull away and alienate ourselves from His love and all He has to offer us when we are intimate with Him. And when we are pulled away from that love, it's like a flower out of water…we start to feel so dry and lifeless in comparison to the way we feel when we are connected fully to Him. Satan wants us to believe that there *is* condemnation. But Jesus promises *no* condemnation and went to great lengths in His short time on earth to make sure we saw Him prove this promise to be true.

The Woman at the Well

John 4 describes a scene that makes this whole idea of no condemnation crystal clear for us as women. It involves Jesus and a Samaritan woman. Jesus was on His way to Galilee from Judea and had to pass through Samaria to get there. In those days, Jews believed Samaritans were "ceremonially unclean." They didn't ascribe to the same set of religious practices as the Jews, so in the minds of the Jewish religious leaders of the day, that meant they were not good enough for many things, including interaction.

Our world today is still full of situations where people are made to feel not good enough for many reasons…for their skin colour, for their gender, for their place of residence, for their beliefs. That kind of discrimination and condemnation really upset Jesus. He did not want people treating one another that way, and He seized every opportunity to make it known to anyone who would listen. Not only did He verbally speak out against that kind of attitude, but even more powerfully, He regularly lived out the *truth* behind His words.

So, Jesus was passing through Samaria. A Jew was passing through an "unclean" place. You would think that if there was truth to the fact that Samaritans were unclean, Jesus would have hustled through there as fast as possible. But He didn't. Even though it was Samaria, He was tired, so He stopped at Jacob's well. Soon after, a Samaritan woman came to the well to draw water. And Jesus spoke to her.

Let's keep track for a second. He stops in an unclean place, by what can only be considered an unclean well (because Samaritans use it), and now He is talking to an unclean woman! In those days, that was not culturally appropriate. Men did not speak to women they did not know, not if they were respectable and concerned about appearance and image, anyway. But Jesus speaks to her. Not only does He speak to her, He asks her to draw Him a drink. Being willing to drink from something a Samaritan has taken a drink from? Jesus is breaking protocol and religious parameters all over the place.

I've often wondered what present-day "religious" practices He would be standing against if He were visibly here among us. I think of some of the things we are so convinced are "right" and "biblical," and I wonder if He would agree. Would He agree that you can't take communion until you have gone through a process? Or would He want anyone who loves Him and accepts His sacrifice to participate? Would He say no to baptizing someone because of their age or the length of time they have been saved, or would He dunk them as soon as they indicate their desire? I know I'm likely making some people uncomfortable, and I'm not trying to slander religious practices per se…I just want to make sure we remember that what Jesus was concerned about was far more heart-centred and focused on *Him* than some of our "right" practices can sometimes be.

The Bible clearly states that Jesus came into this world to save us. Why? Because He *loves* us. Those fundamental facts, which flow from one another— our need for salvation, His love for us and His desire and ability to save us—are the most important things we can ever concern ourselves with. But I know that's not always how it feels. And that's the only reason I raise this point—because I have certainly experienced and witnessed others experiencing condemnation for not following "right" religious practices. I've heard from many people that non-conformity to a certain set of religious practices has brought them heaps of judgment and spiritual woundedness. And I just can't find anywhere in Scripture where Jesus condoned that kind of attitude.

In fact, His whole life was focused on helping people understand there was a better way…His way. That, like it says in Romans 8, we are no longer under the law but are under grace because of Him. Because of His death on the cross. Because He paid the price for us once and for all. Because He showed us that He loves us *so* much, all else pales in comparison. He has saved us from ourselves, from all our human rules and practices of supposed godliness. All He wants in return is our lives surrendered to Him and what He stood for. Which, as far as I can see, boils down ultimately to His love for us and the fact that love is supposed to compel us to love others in such a pure way that they are drawn to Christ. We are to be so smitten with Him and so altered by His love that others see that and want it too. But that's hard to do when we are either condemning others or ourselves.

Back to the woman at the well. He spoke to her. But more than that, He spoke to her knowing her deep, dark, not so pretty secrets. She had had five husbands. Not something a devout, practicing Jew would look favourably upon. And also not in line with Jewish values, she was living with a man who was not her husband. The extent to which Jesus was breaking protocol just went through the thatched roof. Talking to a *Samaritan woman* who was living quite loosely in contrast to Jewish standards. Almighty God loved her enough that He purposely, knowingly and willingly threw all religious and cultural order of the day aside because He was focused on why He came...to show His love to everyone so they could be saved.

According to the rules of her time, if anyone was "deserving" of condemnation, for all intents and purposes that woman was. And more than that, if anyone had the authority to condemn someone for less-than-appropriate behaviour, it would be Jesus. But He didn't do that. Instead, He did the exact opposite. He conveyed in that interaction that she was worth His time. That she had inherent worth and dignity because she was one of His creation. Jesus offered her grace, mercy, compassion and love. She was worth that much to Him.

So that's exactly what He did. He told her that He was the Messiah (the Saviour the Jews were waiting for) and He could give her something that would satisfy her "thirst" forever. Him. The answer to the longing in those deep, soulful places. He told her that He indeed knew her lifestyle...but this gift was still available to her. And what happened?

She went running into town to tell others about who she had just met. That there was this guy who she thought was the Messiah because He knew all about her without her telling Him anything. And He offered her the answer to her life's pain. That got people's attention, so they sought Jesus out. And pretty soon they believed too. They told the woman that they first believed because of what she said, but after they met Him, they believed because of Him. That's what happens when you encounter Jesus and His love...you can't help but be changed by Him, wooed by Him, because of how He is with you. His love is life-changing.

Look at how He was with the Samaritan woman. He didn't condemn her. He had every right to—remember that. But He didn't. He didn't ignore what was wrong, either. He gave the solution to it. That just moves me, and I can't contain the thankfulness that wells up in me. He loves us enough to not leave us in our mess. He doesn't turn away because we are a lost cause. He doesn't shake His head and make us feel shame because we can't seem to conquer that one bad habit. He doesn't jab us with a sarcastic barb to shake us out of our misery. He doesn't make us feel embarrassed in His presence because we are so far from godly.

And He doesn't make excuses for us, either, so that we can continue to behave in the ways that He knows will end in destruction for us. He labels them for what they are, just like He did with the Samaritan woman. Not in a condemning way, but in a factual way. That's true love, isn't it? Loving someone enough to tell them the truth. That's what Jesus does for us, because He *is* truth.

Many well-meaning people think the best thing you can do is to show someone who is in a bad spot "tough love." I have looked high and low through the Bible, and I can't find any stories where Jesus does this when someone is wounded and needing help. Nor have I found a place where He makes someone feel two inches tall after an interaction with Him. Convicted, yes. Insulted and put down, no. Rather, I find story after story of people healed by Him, set free from sin and evil by Him, encouraged to live differently because of His love and made to see clearly because of the clarity He offers them.

The only time I can ever find a record of Jesus condemning people is when they are saying that they are operating in His name yet are *not* showing love, not living out the truth. When they are misrepresenting Him. Like the religious leaders of the day who were walking around condemning everyone for not following the rules as well as they were, even though their hearts were hard to those who needed Jesus. Or those who were making a mockery of Him by using His name, His church and His message for their own gain. Specifically, behaviours that don't accurately represent His love and what He came to do and the purity of faith.

I wonder how He would feel about the way things are today. Would He come across religious leaders today who are misrepresenting Him and His message? Would He be pleased with what He found?

I'd like to touch on one more passage from the Bible that God showed me this morning as I was spending time with Him. He does that often, by the way. He keeps taking me to verses and Bible passages that fit perfectly with the part of the book I am working on or a part that I know is to come. It always blesses me when that happens, because I know that means His hand is on this project. But I share that with you so you can be blessed as well, because what it also means is that He led me to write about it because He wants it for you, too. Because He loves you.

Jude is just a one-chapter book of the Bible, right before Revelation. In verse 24, it says, *"To him who is able to keep you from stumbling and to present you before his glorious presence without fault and with great joy."* This passage is frequently read as a "doxology" or a blessing, often at the end of a church service. And what it says really is a blessing from God to us. But did you notice in the middle the part that is so specific to this chapter? He, meaning Jesus, is able to present *you* without fault. That verse says that because of Him, we stand in His presence (now and in heaven) and are seen as having *no* fault.

Because of Jesus, we are seen by Him as clean. *Without* fault. *No* condemnation. It doesn't say that He will present us before His glorious presence wishing we were good enough. It doesn't say that He will present us before His glorious presence even though we have faults. Or that He can't present us before His glorious presence because of our faults. Because of Jesus' love and sacrifice for us, in His eyes we don't have fault. Not because of us; because of Him. And we are presented with great joy. I've tried to decide whether the great joy is ours because we are without fault or His because He gets to present us without fault— and I've decided that, really, either interpretation is just as precious.

A Personal Reflection

The perfection of this plan brings me to tears every time I spend any time reflecting upon it. Tears of joy and thankfulness. He knows me. He knows that I am, by nature, a perfectionist. And also, by nature, I'm unable to attain that perfectionistic standard set for myself, by myself. I spent a good part of my younger life feeling self-condemnation because of that. Expecting myself to be perfect and really being hard on myself when I didn't measure up.

My perfectionistic standards prevented me from doing many things...or else I did them, but with great anxiety. I expected myself to get As. That's it. Anything less than an A was not good enough. I pushed myself so hard to attain that, and for the most part, I succeeded—even in post-secondary education. But it was not worth it at all. I think back to how stressful life was because of that expectation, and I wish I could go back and help my younger self understand the truth I'm sharing with you here, because it would have saved me years of stress and unnecessary strain.

I also expected myself to look perfect. So there was a time in my life when I would eat very little. Or eat a lot and take some laxatives to deal with what I ate. I even made myself throw up sometimes when I felt so disgusted with myself for having had such poor self-control. These self-destructive behaviours never became a pattern for me; nor did they become engrained in my lifestyle to the point that they took over and consumed me. But there was a time in my late teen years when I was tempted to use them from time to time, and the fact that I dabbled in them on and off illustrates that I was not thinking properly about myself. If I had the body now at 40 that I had at 19, I'd be thrilled!! God thankfully showed me the truth about my worth in my very early twenties and freed me from this unrealistic expectation of myself that led to daily self-condemnation and some unhealthy behaviours at times.

I know I'm not the only one who has struggled in this way, which is why I'm sharing this with you now. The only person who knew this about me before I wrote this part of the chapter was my husband. I'm sharing so you know I'm not perfect, and because I'm free from condemnation, I can share my "failures" publicly without fear of condemnation. Sort of "proof," if you will, that I am truly free. Because if I was not free from condemnation, I would be worried about being judged for admitting to those struggles. Not that some of you won't judge me—you will. But that doesn't bother me anymore. Because I truly understand that there is no condemnation in Christ Jesus, so I'm okay with not being perceived as perfect anymore. (Do you hear the lie I used to believe? That these things made me seem perfect? I can hear the lie, loud and clear.)

I also share it so you know that this no-condemnation stuff isn't just some theory I've never had opportunity to practically apply in my own life. I've struggled. I've lived both sides of what I'm writing about...the self-condemnation side and the no-condemnation side. And the no-condemnation side is *way* better, so I want it for you as well.

Maybe you can't relate to my personal example. We are all unique. And some people are blessed with fewer traps in this area of their lives. They are able to let go and not condemn self and others more easily than other people are. If that's you, take a moment and thank God for that tremendous blessing in your life, because it truly is one. For those of you who have read this chapter and are noticing that God is tugging at you about areas of your life that you have accepted condemnation for, despite what Jesus has done for you, write those areas down somewhere, like that journal we talked about earlier. Then, give them to God. Confess to Him that you have not accepted, until now, that He took care of those "failures" for you already through Jesus. Tell Him that from this moment on you accept that you are free from condemnation because of Jesus. Say that you will no longer accept condemnation as truth, because it is not. Then, claim what the *truth* is about you.

In case you need some help to get going, Neil Anderson has written an amazing list of who we are in Christ that I have included for you in appendix B, with permission. But I also want you to ask God what His truth about you is and write it in your journal as well. Ask Him, and then sit quietly and listen as His Holy Spirit whispers to you. He *will* answer you, because He wants nothing more than intimacy with you and longs for you to know Him and for you to be known by Him. He would love for you to understand how He sees you. Start with

"I am not condemned for my mistakes, and I am not defined by them," and see how He reveals the truth about what He thinks of you from there.

If you ask Him to speak to you, and you don't think He does or all you hear are condemning thoughts, *do not* think this means that God doesn't have anything other than condemnation to offer you. What it actually means is that the enemy of our souls is working really hard to keep you stuck in condemnation. Which means to me, Satan knows that you will be really impactful for the kingdom of God when you are not rendered stuck by condemnation. Neil Anderson says Satan knows he can't change who we are in Christ so he tries to change our perception of it instead. That thought, I think, pairs very nicely with one from Priscilla Shirer in *A Jewel in His Crown,* which states that Satan knows that if he can get us focused enough on our weaknesses, we will never get around to using our strengths for the kingdom of God.

Think about that for a second. If you weren't so consumed by the things you think are failures, the things you feel make you not good enough, what *would* you be consumed with? We'll talk a lot more about these ideas later on. But for now, I point this out so that you don't get discouraged, and so you realize that you don't have to stay stuck. I suggest that you reach out to God (again) about this. It may mean that He will lead you to speak to a trusted Christian friend, counsellor or pastor to help you address this "stuckness" you are feeling. Or it may mean that in your quietness with Him, He will open your eyes to how you have been lured to accept beliefs that are not truth about you, which will be enough to help you break through this attack on your view of yourself so you can feel His love.

Whatever you do, don't give up. Keep listening. He *will* speak to you. Maybe it won't be today. Maybe it will be as you are driving to the store. Maybe it will be as you are falling asleep one night. Maybe you will hear a song and you will feel like He is singing the words directly to you. Don't forget, the Bible says, "*With the Lord a day is like a thousand years, and a thousand years are like a day*" (2 Peter 3:8), so you might think He is not answering you, but He will. And don't worry— I don't think He'll make you wait one thousand years! Ephesians 3:16–18 says,

> I pray that out of his glorious riches he may strengthen you with power through his Spirit in your inner being, so that Christ may dwell in your hearts through faith. And I pray that you, being rooted and established in **love**, may have power, together with all the Lord's holy people, to grasp how wide and long and high and deep is the love of Christ. (emphasis added)

Did you catch what that passage is saying to you? That His love for you is wide, long, high and deep. How will you understand that? By being rooted in His love. Rooted. When we root, or anchor, ourselves in the truth—what the Bible says about His love for us, which means *no* condemnation—we will finally be able to understand just how wide, how long, how high and how deep His love for us truly is. Even a glimpse of that reality has the capacity to overwhelm us...in a good way. In a way that makes a difference. That is life-changing.

I'll end this chapter by telling you about a woman I met whom I will call Sue. Sue was at a woman's retreat where I had the privilege of speaking. The topic was on hearing God's voice. Throughout the weekend, there were several opportunities for the women to break off alone and reflect on their personal reaction to what was being discussed and to listen to what God was saying to them.

Sue asked to speak alone with me at the end of the retreat to share what had happened to her with God on the weekend. Sue said she had ended Saturday evening very angry and upset. Her journaling had been filled with reflections of these strong emotions, largely through self-condemning thoughts and feelings. On the Sunday morning, part of the topic included a discussion about how Satan tries to stop us from hearing God, using some pretty "common" negative feelings about ourselves to do so. Sue said that as I listed some of the accusations Satan commonly uses, she found herself being able to relate to every one of them, and more than that—they were the things she had been writing in her journal in anger the night before.

When she went off on her own on Sunday to listen to God and hear what messages of love He had for her, she found herself flooded with good, warm, loving thoughts about herself that felt completely foreign to the negative self-condemnation that had become the norm for her. She was blown away that once she realized those negative things were lies and that she didn't have to listen to them, she was able to hear the *truth*.

Sue was a little skeptical of the good stuff at first, saying, "I don't know if that was the Holy Spirit or not," because she was not used to hearing Him love her in that way. But it didn't take too long before God affirmed for Sue that of course it was Him. That those words were His truth for her, words He wanted her to accept. And her openness to labelling Satan's lies as what they were enabled her to hear the love message from God that had been truth all along in her life, if only she'd not been so consumed with condemnation. Sue asked God to tell her the truth about how He felt about her, and He did...because God *so* loves Sue. Just like He *so* loves you.

CHAPTER THREE

Love Means Freedom

The Spirit of the Sovereign LORD is on me, because the LORD has anointed me to proclaim good news to the poor. He has sent me to bind up the brokenhearted, to proclaim freedom for the captives and release from darkness for the prisoners.

Isaiah 61:1

I can still remember a time when I was a little girl and I'd been sent to my room for doing something wrong. I can't remember what I had done, but I *do* remember my mom coming into my room afterwards to talk with me about my misbehaviour. I grew up in a Christian home, in a family that attended church a minimum of four different times in a week (three on Sunday and at least once during the week for Bible study), so I was very aware of how important my parents' faith was to them. In my childish wisdom, I thought perhaps if I spiritualized the situation, my mom might take pity on me and see me as somewhat of a helpless victim of Satan (instead of disobedient) and hopefully lessen my punishment. So when she came into my room to talk with me and asked why I did "it" (whatever "it" was), I looked up at her with my biggest, saddest little girl eyes and said, "Mommy, the devil made me do it!" To which she very sternly responded, "The devil, *my foot!*"

I think my understanding of the reality of and theology behind spiritual warfare has grown since then, and that's what I'll focus on for the next little while. I realize there are a lot of views on this topic and the degree to which it plays a part in our day-to-day functioning. Ideas that range from complete denial of any spiritual battle going on at all to living in fear of Satan and his schemes. Far be it from me to attempt to suggest that you need to switch to my way of thinking. After all, this is between you and God.

My worldview on this topic is this: the Bible is very clear—there *is* a spiritual battle going on, and it is for our freedom. As a result, I will outline what the Bible says about this topic and how I think it impacts us on a day-to-day basis. I will then address how this topic relates to how much we are loved.

Deep, Soulful Places

What the Bible Says

Ephesians 6:12 says, *"For our struggle is not against flesh and blood, but against the rulers, against the authorities, against the powers of this dark world and against the spiritual forces of evil in the heavenly realms."* That is one of the clearest verses in the Bible indicating there *is* a battle going on—not one that is human to human (although, unfortunately, there are many of those also), but one occurring in the spiritual world. This deserves our attention because, I believe, this battle is at the root of so much that gets in the way of our understanding about God's love for us. This battle is at the root of many of the conflicts we experience with others. It is at the root of so much of what we think is wrong about ourselves. It is at the root of what immobilizes us and makes us feel "less than."

As a result, it is very important to talk about this issue of spiritual warfare, because God promises us freedom—and yet countless Christians (many whom are very godly and devoted) are stuck. Immobilized. Prisoners to things we as Christians shouldn't theoretically be prisoners to. Things you would expect you would be free from when you are bathed in God's love.

And that's because this battle for our freedom is about Satan doing everything in his power to keep us stuck. Everything in his power. His power is way less than God's, but make no mistake, he's pretty powerful. The Bible describes him as the ruler of this world (John 12:31). We need to be clear about who our enemy is. Battle Tactics 101 involves understanding who your enemy is so you are armed and prepared for the attack. It's hard to ready yourself for battle if you don't know what or whom you are battling. People make whole careers out of studying enemy tactics, because it is critical to the success of a battle. Profiling, for the FBI, CIA, provincial police forces and the Royal Mounted Police, is a crucial component to solving crime. Why? Because when you have a sense of who you are looking for, it makes it a whole lot easier to spot him (or her) and figure out what his next step is so you can stop him. It is wise for us to understand who *our* enemy is so we can spot him when he is at work. So we don't unintentionally accept something as truth when it's really an enemy attack. So we don't find ourselves imprisoned when we are supposed to be free.

Our enemy is content to keep us stuck in whatever will best prevent us from feeling or being free. It could be a thought. It could be a behaviour. It could be a situation. It could be in the past. It could be in the present. Because of God's love, there is no condemnation, but our enemy wants you to think there still is. Because you can't feel freedom and condemnation at the same time. See how subtle that is? He doesn't have to get you to commit some major "crime" or "sin"—he just has to make you feel guilty about something or unforgiven. Not good enough. And then he has you.

Because ultimately, this battle for our freedom exists *because* of God's life-changing love for us. Satan knows how powerful it is for you and me to truly understand the depth and breadth of God's love for us and how it has the capacity to fill those deep, soulful places…so he works very hard to prevent that from happening.

This isn't just a theory that makes a good subject for theological debate; it is real life. There is a spiritual battle going on that we are a part of as Christians. Isaiah 61:1 is an Old Testament prophecy of what the Messiah would come to do, later quoted by Jesus in the Gospels (Luke 4:18) as His mission for His time here on earth. Notice what He says—He came to bring release from darkness for the prisoners. Many Christians believe this refers to the act of salvation, that by defeating Satan through His death on the cross Jesus has brought release from darkness for the prisoners. Which is 100 percent true. But this idea of freedom isn't just about salvation. It is also about sanctification, the process of us being made more and more like Jesus as we grow closer in our relationship to Him, deepen our understanding of who He is, and are changed by His presence in our lives. Our release from darkness is involved in that process as well.

We *are* free, from an eternal perspective, as soon as we accept what Jesus did for us on the cross (please see appendix E if you are not clear about what exactly I'm referring to). That salvation is secure, and the Bible says in Romans 8:38–39 that *nothing* can separate us from the love of God in Christ Jesus. Nothing. But if you notice, Isaiah 61:1 (a.k.a. Jesus' mission on earth) is about more than that. It also says He came to bind up the broken-hearted. He loves us *so* much that He cares about the hurts in our lives and wants us to be healed from them. He offers in relationship with Him a place where those hurts can be left, where *they do not define us* or hold us down. So we can *feel* free.

He wants to heal us from the abuses we've endured as children and adults— the struggles in our marriages, the abandonment we feel, the behaviour problems with our children, the problems in our friendships—and He wants us to know that our worth remains and His love for us is secure, regardless of the broken hearts we may be carrying. Satan wants us to stay stuck as prisoners to those things. But that is not what Jesus promises in relationship with Him. He came to take care of more than just our salvation. He came to release us from all kinds of darkness so we are truly free.

Deep, Soulful Places

Unfortunately, the ruler of this world is very powerful in his persuasions, and many of us have bought into the lies designed to keep us prisoners to feelings of inadequacy, inferiority and worthlessness, lies that prevent us from fully understanding how cherished we are, and why.

Why Satan Bothers with Us

You may have been wondering, "Why does Satan bother with *me?*" Because Satan knows how God has gifted you and understands all too well what an impact you can, will and do make in the world around you when you feel fully free in Christ to use the beauty, love and talents God has given you. And he knows that the more stuck we are, the less likely we are to feel free to obey God, to take the risks He asks us to take with Him and for Him. Because we are too focused on the bars of the prison around us.

Think about that for a moment, and maybe get your journal so you can jot down what comes to mind as you reflect. Are there things in your life that you see as weaknesses or inadequacies that are prison bars keeping you from using your strengths for the kingdom of God? What would you be doing that you aren't doing now if Satan didn't have you convinced to stay stuck? What risk would you be taking for God that you don't think you are capable of taking right now? I wouldn't be writing this book if I was listening to the enemy, I can tell you that much. The enemy has been loud and clear and quite persistent in his efforts to make me stop, to say the least.

Another reason why Satan is on the attack is because this is about way more than just you and me. It's about the ultimate war between good and evil that we read about in Ephesians. And because you have chosen to align yourself with the good side, you are an enemy to the evil one, and he wants you out of his way. Satan is looking to lessen Christ's army (or disarm it) and increase his. It appears that Satan still hasn't accepted his defeat; and although he knows he doesn't stand a fighting chance, the enemy of our souls just loves to mess with God's people because he actually understands better than we do just how cherished we are. And therefore he understands just how much it hurts God's heart to see His children in prison, suffering, feeling unloved, unfulfilled and unable to live the way God intended for them to live. It's about inflicting pain. I can think of countless women I have worked with over the years who have fled horrendous abuse. When an abuser knows that he has lost control and power over a woman, he doesn't like it. So he uses the children to get at the mom. Why? Because he knows the best way to get revenge and inflict pain on her is not to attack her directly—it's to attack what matters most to her, her children. It's like Satan is the abusive partner, and he knows he's lost his partner; she's gone for good. But he won't go down without a fight. So he goes after the kids—us.

First Peter 5:8 says, "*Be of sober spirit, be on the alert. Your adversary, the devil, prowls about like a roaring lion, seeking someone to devour*" (NASB). Why would he seek someone to devour? Because he is angry! Why is he angry? Because he is a sore loser! Like a bully in the schoolyard, he doesn't like his power to be taken away from him, so he lashes out and looks for his next victim because he is mad at the world. Most of the time with schoolyard bullies, you can look at their lives and gain some understanding into why they have so much anger and hatred inside that they treat others with disrespect. It's rare that there is not some sort of substantial dysfunction at the root of the bullying.

We just have to look to the cross to understand why Satan is so mad, why he is being such a bully and retaliating all over the place in the lives of those who love Jesus. Satan has had his power taken away (from an eternal standpoint). He's not going to get what he wants (to rule the world and be God), and he knows it. So he's decided to hit below the belt and try to hurt those who love God, because he is *fully* aware that we are *so* loved. And he is aware of what us being *so* loved means to his attempts to rule the world, and he doesn't want to see that come to fruition as God intended.

I don't know about you, but that makes me annoyed with the enemy! I feel like saying, "Go prowl elsewhere! You don't belong here with me—I'm not yours to mess with!" And, to a certain extent, that is exactly what we are supposed to do. We need to be aware that this spiritual battle is going on, because it is. But that doesn't mean we should live in fear; nor does it mean we get to abdicate our responsibility and blame everything on Satan (as I tried to with my mom). What it does mean is that we need to understand *how* this battle is specifically going on in our lives so we can claim our authority in Christ and live in the freedom that is ours as a result.

Not giving consideration to the spiritual battle in our lives is like leaving the trenches during a war to go for a leisurely stroll in enemy territory.

Enemy Tactics

Satan can't change who we are in Christ, so he tries to distract us from that truth instead, which to me reinforces that Satan *does* actually know he has already lost the battle for our souls as Christians. He knows that when we are in Christ, we are Christ's. And we are Christ's *forever.* Jeremiah 31:3 says, "*I have loved you with an everlasting love"* (NASB). God's love for us will never change, and Satan understands that. But he's not content to back down. So he comes at things from another angle. Not an angle with an eternal impact on our salvation, but certainly one with a temporal—while we are here on earth—impact. I can't tell you how Satan will try to distract you from the truth, because his method is case specific…he studies us, watches us, and then finds the chink in the armour and goes for that little (or big) hole. You may be thinking you don't know what that hole is. Please don't fear, and please don't put down your weapon and surrender. With the help of the Holy Spirit, you can know the areas where you are either in prison or tempted to enter into prison.

What I *can* tell you is that Satan is merciless. He will use whatever he thinks is a weakness and will twist it for his gain. Shame, self-doubt and accusation are classic tactics of his, and they very often work. Remember our discussion about no condemnation? Condemnation is a prison. Satan loves to plague us with self-condemning thoughts—and he loves to twist what others say so that we feel outwardly condemned. He also enjoys convincing someone else to join the party and condemn us too.

Capitalizing on the effect of childhood victimization and abuse is another major way he keeps us bound and ineffective. I have worked with many people who because of abuse believe horrible lies about themselves, their worth, their bodies, or God's care for them. Victimization and trauma are perfect breeding grounds for the lies of the enemy to fester and grow so that he can keep us blind to the truth that God has for us. He loves to convince victims of trauma that it was their fault. That they are "less than" because of what was inflicted upon them. That somehow it happened to them because they deserved it. Lies. A prison. A very effective way to keep people completely bound up.

False guilt is his frequent weapon of choice. God designed the feeling of guilt to be our internal check to help us know when we have strayed from the right path. The God-given feeling of guilt, *real* guilt, is actually positive, because it is the pathway to change, through forgiveness and healing. False guilt, however, is a key way Satan keeps us in prison. You can know you are feeling false guilt if you continue to feel shame, self-doubt and condemnation after you have confessed your sins to Christ or if the guilt is about something of which you were or are the victim. Guilt is supposed to liberate us and open the door to freedom through repentance and forgiveness, not keep us stuck.

Let's stop for a minute and reflect on the following questions. These are questions that I have had to ask myself many times. How does Satan try to undermine your life for Christ? Keep in mind, a satanic attack doesn't just involve temptation to commit "big" sins. I'm asking you to search yourself, with the help of the Holy Spirit, to discern whether or not there is a chink in the armour…a way that Satan has managed to hem you in, into your own personal little prison.

For example: is it through a spirit of fear, anger, jealousy, anxiety or pride? Is it through relying on yourself instead of God? Is it by encouraging you to minimize your strengths and focus instead on your weaknesses? Is it by getting you to focus your worth on your body shape or complexion? Is it by twisting the truth so that you doubt God's good intentions for your life? Is it by convincing you to believe that you deserve continual punishment for forgiven wrongs? Is it through a temptation to overeat, starve yourself, or binge and purge? Is it through an impulse towards drugs, alcohol or food to numb the pain instead of turning to God? Or is it through searching for your worth and security in relationships with men?

There are so many ways the enemy can subtly find his way in. Ways we think are us, part of our personality, not him. Ways that are so mainstream in society that we don't catch on that they are actually underground enemy tactics. It would be clear that it was part of Satan's arsenal if it fit with our Hollywood idea about how Satan works—but often his attacks masquerade as everyday life, so they go undetected and unthwarted. He's like a double agent—we don't realize it's the enemy, so we don't do anything about his presence in our day-to-day lives.

I have witnessed over the years that although every child of God is aligned against the enemy, there are certain times in the life of a Christian when it would appear that Satan is working even harder to bring him or her down.[2] Since he doesn't need to worry about those who aren't a threat to his purposes, he will be concentrating on anyone seeking to live their life in a way that is pleasing to God. Lukewarm Christians seem to be of less concern to the enemy. I assume that is because they are not making headway for the kingdom of God, so they are less of a threat to Satan's efforts to rule the world. But those who are actively living their lives for Christ, trying hard to grow closer to Him…well, they are on the front lines, and they will be a focus for the enemy. Witnessing to non-Christians, changing your life around for Christ, growing in Christ, obeying Christ and what He is calling you to do…those are all direct threats to the enemy, and he will see them as such and respond accordingly.

---

[2] See Chip Ingram, *The Invisible War: What Every Believer Needs to Know about Satan, Demons and Spiritual Warfare* (Grand Rapids: Baker Books, 2006).

Deep, Soulful Places

I'm Not Feeling *So* Loved Right Now!

For some of you, I've said nothing you haven't already heard a million times before. You are so well versed in this area of spiritual warfare, you have just been reading along, nodding in silent agreement. Some of you may think I am way off base, and you totally disagree. Some of you, however, may be questioning if it's worth aligning yourself with Christ if this is what you have to look forward to. You may be thinking it's easier to just not choose sides or to just stay in the lukewarm category so you are not waving a red cloth in front of a bull. Don't let the enemy deceive you into thinking those thoughts are truth. They are not.

I remember working with a teenage boy some years ago who lived in a part of town known for significant gang activity. He was really struggling with anxiety, so I wondered if it was related to gang pressures. I will never forget his answer when I asked him if he was involved in a gang. He said, "Even if you choose to not be in a gang, you are choosing to be in a gang." He went on to explain that by not aligning yourself with one of the gangs, you were in effect saying you were against the gang, since you were not with them.

The same is true in the spiritual world around us. There are only two sides. There is no neutral territory. Jesus said, *"Whoever is not with me is against me"* (Luke 11:23). By not aligning yourself with Christ, thinking that will keep you on neutral ground, you are choosing the other side. And even lukewarm Christians have chosen a side; they just aren't as active in the battle, so they are farther down on the hit list. But they have still chosen a side. In fact, I would argue that their lukewarm stance is likely a result of some previous enemy attack, some sort of deceptive tactic that has them lulled into complacency.

The reality is, we are safest when we are closest to God, even though that makes us the greatest threat to Satan, because we are on the winning side! Satan has already been defeated on the cross. Don't forget that. *He has already lost.* So we do not need to be afraid. I realize this might seem as though I'm contradicting myself. I just spent a great deal of time building the case for why we need to understand the enemy of our souls and the battle we face and that we need to recognize his attacks because he is trying to imprison us… and then in the next breath I'm saying Satan has been defeated and we do not need to be afraid.

Those two statements are not contradictory, believe it or not! It's true—we do need to be aware of the spiritual battle that exists, but we don't need to be afraid, because as Christians we have the authority we need in Christ Jesus to be armed for the battle. Jesus doesn't leave us in this battle unarmed and alone. He doesn't woo us into His family with His love and then leave us for the wolves.

Isaiah 61 says He came to set the prisoners free. *Free.* Our authority in Christ, through the power of the Holy Spirit, gives us what we need to be prepared for the battle and to live in the freedom He promises.

Ephesians 6:10–11 says, *"Finally, be strong in the Lord and in his mighty power. Put on the full armor of God, so that you can take your stand against the devil's schemes."* Notice, here it is *God's* armour that enables us to stand against the devil's schemes. He gives us *His* armour to protect us. We aren't just on the winning side; we have access to all of the hero's best armour to keep us safe while we stand on the winning side.

Because Satan is a defeated foe, he has no authority over us. He has the ability to influence us, but he has no authority over us. In fact, in Christ, we have authority over Satan! In John 14:12 Jesus tells His disciples they will be able to do what He has been doing (miracles, healing, casting out demons) when He leaves them, because the Spirit of God will be left to help. So that means His authority over the enemy is ours, because of the Holy Spirit in our lives. Satan will put up a fight and make it seem as though we are powerless against him, but we are not.

When Jesus was casting out demons in the Gospels, they even put up a fight with *Him* and didn't always leave the first time He told them to. Satan has no problem trying to deceive, and he seems to not even have a problem with trying to get away with not listening to Jesus, of all people! He wants us to forget that he was already defeated at the cross and would rather that we feel enslaved to whatever it is that is keeping us imprisoned. Jesus came to set us free—eternally and temporally, to bind up the broken-hearted (and all the lies of Satan that go along with that woundedness) and to bring release from darkness for the prisoners. We are not fighting this battle for our victory. Our victory is already won because of Jesus. We are fighting this battle to stand our ground *in* our victory.

In John 8:32, the Bible says, *"You will know the truth, and the truth will make you free"* (NASB). The *truth* is that Jesus Christ died for us and defeated Satan, and when we claim our freedom in Christ that is ours to claim by the power of the Holy Spirit, Satan and his helpers *have* to listen to us. The Bible has given some very helpful truths to guide us as we deal with this battle.

One way to stand our ground, to claim our authority in Christ, is found in Colossians 3:2, which says, *"Set your mind on the things above, not on the things that are on earth"* (NASB). This means focusing our hearts, minds and bodies on the things God says are important and of value. That sounds like a typical churchy explanation, so let me go a bit further. It means going before God and asking Him to reveal to us our areas of vulnerability and then, instead of getting bogged down and overwhelmed by them (condemnation), giving them right back to Him for His strength, help and healing. And it means that any time we get that heavy, down, stuck feeling, instead of embracing it and giving into it as the truth in our lives, we examine what it is and where it is coming from, to see if it is in fact truth or a lie. It means we pay attention to the things we allow into our minds, hearts and souls. That we don't dabble in the other side, playing with fire, to open doors to things that should really be kept out, things that are not of God. And remember, if they are not of God, they are of someone else—the enemy.

Things like New Age theology, spiritists, fortune tellers, tarot card readers, tea leaf readings and smudging are not from above—they are things from the earth. Things like idol worship, trance encounters, talking with the dead, and mainstream activities—TV shows, movies and video games—that glorify this type of activity and are growing in their acceptance and popularity are not of God. They are door openers to the side that seeks to kill and destroy, that prowls around like a lion. You don't want to leave your front door open to the enemy of your soul. So you need to shut it to the things of this world that could do just that. Remember bloody Mary in the school bathroom with the lights off? Remember Dungeons and Dragons as an afterschool club? Remember reading your horoscope to see if that cute boy would ask you out? Things of this earth, not of God. Door openers to the enemy. And so one way we can protect ourselves is to keep ourselves away from those things. Keep the door closed.

I also think that verse in Colossians speaks to how powerfully the Bible can protect our minds from the lies of the enemy. God's word is power. It is sharper than any two-edged sword (Hebrews 4:12). And it is *truth.* So it never lies. It never leads us astray. In fact, in John 1 it talks about how the Word of God was with God, and the Word was God. And He (the Word, Jesus) dwelt among us, and we beheld His glory, the glory of the only begotten Son of the Father, full of grace and *truth.* God's Word is powerful—it is in God. It is embodied in Jesus and the life He lived, because He was and is *truth.* And so He, the *truth,* will set you free.

When we focus on what His Word says about us, this world and how we are to live our lives, we can protect ourselves from going down the wrong path. When we are confronted with the lies of the enemy and we look to the Bible to see if we can find the lies there, and we can't, we have the power to cut through the fog and see clearly what the *truth* is. This exercise is especially helpful when the enemy's attack is negative thoughts about yourself, about God or about His ability to handle a situation. In those times, if we compare the thoughts we are thinking with what the Bible says about us, we can effectively snuff out the lies of the enemy. The "In Christ" list in appendix B is very helpful for this. There are over 30 statements taken directly from verses in the Bible about who we are in Christ. Any thoughts or feelings about ourselves not found on that list can be rejected; they are lies that just aren't true of children of God and are designed to render us ineffective for God's glory.

We need to be clear about who the real enemy is. It isn't ourselves, our bodies, our trauma or even the people who profess to love us, and it isn't God. Otherwise we will be so distracted that we won't notice the real enemy undermining us and orchestrating our demise.

So, How Does This Relate to Being *So* Loved?

In John 14, Jesus tells His disciples that He won't leave them as orphans. The Father will send the Spirit—the same Spirit who was the power behind the creation of the world, Jesus' conception and His resurrection from the dead—who will be with them and help them. Why would Jesus say that to the disciples if all that mattered was salvation? If the only thing God wanted to do to show us His love for us was save us from an eternity in hell (which is an amazing act of love in and of itself!), He could have sent Jesus to die and that would be that. But like we've already discussed, because God *so* loves us…because He *cherishes* us…He's also concerned with our here and now. He knows there is a spiritual battle raging, and He wants us to know that He hasn't left us to fight for ourselves, without any help or defense. He wants us to know that He loves us so much that He's taken care of our protection and already arranged for us to have the help we need to live the life we have been given in the way He hopes we will live it.

When you love someone, you are there for that person. When you love someone, you care about that person's safety. When you love someone, if that person needs you, you respond. When you love someone, especially when you are also responsible for that person (like in a parent-child relationship), you make sure that person's needs are met and the person is provided for. When you love someone, you don't ignore important parts of that person's life—you take all of life into consideration. And if you love someone and you know for a fact that person may encounter difficulty, you make sure you help the person with or through that difficulty. Because when you love someone, if that person hurts, you hurt.

God knew the spiritual battle we just talked about would rage…because He knows Satan better than anyone. And He loves us *so* much that He made our continued protection during the battle part of His master plan. Because He knew if He didn't account for that and left us unprotected in the middle of a battle, we would feel trapped, alone and afraid. If we don't feel protected, safe, secure and taken care of, we won't feel the fullness of the love that He has for us. So, knowing the battle would be there, Jesus made sure His disciples knew they would be provided for. Because they were loved. Because we are loved.

Second Corinthians 3:17 says, *"Now the Lord is the Spirit, and where the Spirit of the Lord is, there is freedom."* He left us His Spirit…because the Spirit brings us freedom. And that freedom is a reflection of God's love for us, because you don't leave someone you love trapped. You don't leave someone you love as unsuspecting prey for a merciless predator. You don't leave someone you love alone and defenseless, period. The Spirit brings us our freedom, out of the Father's deep and unending love for us. Because He doesn't want us trapped. Because He doesn't want us to be unsuspecting victims of Satan's devious schemes. Because He doesn't want to see us in pain and tormented, so He died to set us free…*now* and for eternity.

In fact, this protection of our freedom *now* is of such importance to God that it is a theme throughout the messages to the churches that were established after Jesus' death and resurrection. If salvation was all that mattered to God, the whole New Testament would be focused on that, instead of addressing salvation *plus* all the stuff that comes after. The New Testament books of the Bible are full of instructions and encouragements for the new churches about how they were to practically live out their new faith in Christ, part of which was reminding them that they didn't have to try to do that without help. Including the fact that they would be given protection against evil…and help to get and stay free.

Remember 1 Corinthians 13, the description of love we talked about as we started this journey together? Verse 7 says love always protects. Understanding that there is a spiritual battle going on in this world is directly connected to love because it is something we need to be protected from, and love always does that. It always protects. And we are *so* loved. Second Thessalonians 3:3 says, *"But the Lord is faithful, and He will strengthen and protect you from the evil one"* (NASB). Because He loves us, He will *always* protect us from our most dangerous enemy.

But His protection doesn't mean we lose the chance to be part of a real life— which is why He didn't just put us away somewhere safe until He returns to take us to heaven with Him. Some people think that if God really loved us, He'd prevent all bad things from happening to us. And as a parent, I understand why that logic exists. Because, certainly, as a parent I don't want anything bad to happen to my kids. And I sure do everything in my power to protect them from whatever

I have capacity to protect them from. But if I were to shelter them too much, they wouldn't feel loved. They'd feel smothered. They wouldn't be thankful for my preventative behaviours. They'd be resentful. Why? Because as humans, part of what feels loving is to be trusted enough and cared for enough to be given the skills to navigate life and then to be offered freedom to use what we've been given. Freedom to make our own choices. Freedom to be who we are made to be. Freedom to live. So, rather than putting us in some holding cell until heaven to protect us, God offers us freedom and protection for what we most desperately need protection from, in the form of His powerful Spirit Himself.

It feels to me that He is saying, "I love you so much that I'm going to make sure you are protected from evil—for eternity and for your time on earth. I'll give you what you need, through the power of My Spirit, so you can discern the devil's evil schemes, recognize them as lies and deception, and resist him. Claim your authority in My Son over him. And I will give you My truth, so you can be grounded and rooted in it. I will protect you because I love you. But I'm going to do it in a way that you are free—free to be who I made you to be. Free to understand Me. Free to learn about this world I made. Free to make mistakes along the way, but secure in My love nevertheless. Free to live in the world I made for you, but protected from the destruction that awaits it without Me. Free from the hooks Satan will try to sink into you through his lies, because My Spirit will shine His light of truth on those attempts against you. Like a parent who loves their child, I want you to be safe, and I want you to be free. That is why I gave you My Spirit…so you are never alone, and so you have everything you need to be free." That's not taken from a specific passage in the Bible. It's just how I feel the truths of the Bible translate into a present-day reality about this concept of freedom and protection.

From beginning to end, the Bible is clear about God's promises regarding the freedom, and therefore protection, of those He loves. When you love someone, you don't want them to be captive to anything that is not good for them. You don't want them negatively influenced by anyone or anything. You will do whatever it takes to protect them and secure their freedom. Which is exactly how God feels about us. That's why Jesus died for us—and it's why the Father sent His Holy Spirit to indwell us. Because He wants us free.

What If I Don't *Feel* Free?

Spiritual warfare is not my area of expertise. I don't pretend to have all the answers. I'll confess to you now, I wrestled with even writing this chapter. I don't like not knowing things. I don't like not having it all figured out. I would rather not do something at all if I can't do it well. Can you hear the lies of the enemy underneath those statements? I can. And so it feels counterintuitive for me to address a subject in which I can't feel professionally competent. But this is one of those times where I'm being obedient, trusting that God has a plan for this chapter that doesn't need my expertise.

I *do* know, however, that it is actually quite a common Christian experience to love God deeply and know all about Him and His love, promises and goodness but still feel stuck, unloved and bound by something unrelenting and unwilling to let go. To feel like a captive, despite all the *truth* you believe with your whole heart. I also know that many Christians wrestle with this battle even after they have done lots of work in the form of prayer, Bible study, memorization of Scripture and claiming God's truths in their lives. People who have done some very important forms of "freedom taking" and renouncing. People who know God intimately and deeply and yet can't figure out why they don't *feel* free. I've talked to those people, both in my personal life and in my professional life. It's a reality. You may feel you fall into that category. *You are not alone.* God's promise of protection and freedom *does* apply to you as well, despite those feelings of being captive to someone or something.

I have heard some people say that if you feel that way, you aren't really a Christian, because the Bible says that in Christ you are a new creature...the old has passed away, and He has made all things new. I don't agree. I agree with the Bible verse, just not with that interpretation of it. I've heard some people say that with the Holy Spirit in you, you have everything you need to conquer old sin habits and live the way God wants you to. Which is true, but I don't think it is always quite so simple. The implication here is that if you are not feeling able to conquer your sins, maybe there is something wrong with *you*—you are not surrendering enough to Him. You are not doing enough of those spiritual disciplines to help renew you. The problem is with you. Although there are obviously times when this is the case (like in the life of someone who *isn't* seeking to change through the power of the Holy Spirit), I disagree with this when it comes to those people who are genuine in their desire to change and are seemingly doing all the right things to get there. Here I go being heretical again. But I've talked to far too many desperate godly people to accept this interpretation.

When we are in Christ, we are a new creation. The old *has* passed away, and He has made all things new. He owns us. We are His. He is in us, and we are in Him. We are His children, and we are secure in Him forever. His Holy Spirit indwells us, and we have access to the power that comes with the Holy Spirit, so we can live our lives the way He wants us to. Amen? But, if you are struggling to conquer a sin pattern in your life or are feeling trapped in a prison of the enemy, I don't think that means you aren't a Christian. And I also don't think it always means you aren't surrendering enough to Him. What I have learned is that sometimes the level of spiritual warfare can take things into a different realm, requiring a different level of intervention than many well-meaning Christians have ever considered.

This may be making you nervous. *What is she suggesting?* I don't mean to say that we can lose our salvation or that something has the ability to nullify the Holy Spirit's power. Please, do not let the enemy twist my words. That is not what the Bible says.

Let's pretend you have inherited a vacation property someplace warm and beautiful. You can't believe it's yours. It is located exactly where you would want it to be and is decorated to your standards. If it were for sale, you would buy it. But you don't have to. It was given to you, for free. You inherited it—it's legal and it's final. You are *thrilled.* For the first few years of your ownership, you use it often. You set aside as much time as possible to be there. Every time you leave, you can't wait to return. You take great care to keep it in pristine condition. Over time, however, you get busy. You can't get down as often as you'd like, and you don't like it being unoccupied for so long, so you decide to allow others to use your place.

At first, you only allow close friends and family. When you go down after they have been there, things aren't left exactly as you would like them, but close enough, so you let it go. Sometimes your friends and family tell you that when they arrived, it seemed like someone else had been in there. But you don't give this much thought, since you are the owner, the holder of the key. You don't consider that perhaps the previous owner didn't leave you all the keys or didn't collect all the keys he had given out to his friends before he passed it on to you.

After a while your family and friends can't get to your vacation home as frequently, so you decide to rent it out. You place an ad and soon begin to hear from interested renters. You are careful, you think. You check references. You only allow a certain caliber of person to rent from you. And for the most part, aside from a twinge of nervousness, you feel this is okay.

The time comes for you to go for *your* vacation. You are ecstatic. It has been far too long since you got to spend some quality time there. You drive up the drive, and you think, *Hmm...I don't remember it looking quite this "used."* But, it's been a while, and you've been paying someone else to tend to the grounds, so you assume you are just being picky. You unlock the front door, and there's a smell that you don't remember. Not a horrible smell…just the unfamiliar smell of others. You notice that the furniture has been moved a bit. It's not where you left it, and it's not necessarily where you want it. You feel a surge of disappointment that people didn't treat your home as you would treat it.

You carry your suitcase through to the bedroom. Now you start becoming aware that things are not right. It's not just the fact that the bed is slightly disheveled. It's this sense that maybe this isn't really your room…it feels foreign. Like someone else's. You tell yourself that's silly. It's *your* room. It's *your* property! There has been no change in the ownership of the place. But, you begin to wonder, has letting others use it compromised it in some way?

In the kitchen, your inkling turns into a certainty. None of the cutlery is where it belongs. Things are everywhere. You begin to regret ever renting it out. You wonder how you could have been so silly as to think you could open up your home to strangers without being there to oversee things and expect them to treat your property with the kind of care with which you would treat it. You realize you have been playing with fire. You have opened the door to an unwelcome consequence— something that wasn't clear to you when you began renting. And now, you wish you could turn back the hand of time. Start fresh. But the damage has been done. Every drawer displays evidence of now unwelcome guests. Every room bears the mark of someone other than the owner. There is no evidence of forced entry. The entry was granted, but the effects are far more devastating than you expected.

Then you hear a noise coming from the bathroom. You gingerly push open the door. The window is wide open. It has been left open for weeks, since the last renter was in. You get a feeling of dread in the pit of your stomach because you know what this means. There is enough wildlife around your vacation home that you can rest assured there are actually extra visitors in your house, hiding in the dark spaces, trying to keep their presence a secret so they won't be exposed. Your mind races at all the possible vermin and reptiles that may be hiding under beds, in cupboards and behind furniture. An open window! How could they have been so foolish? Isn't it obvious that when you leave open a door or a window, you will get unwanted guests? Squatters that don't own the home but have taken up residence because they've been given a way in. You feel almost defeated as you think about how long it will take to get rid of them all. You wonder how often this has happened. You begin to wonder if this home, that you own, will ever feel like yours again.

Then, just when you think it couldn't get any worse, the front door (that you locked after you came inside) opens. And in walks a stranger! You demand to know who he is and what he is doing in *your* home. He looks at you with equal indignation and tells you that he has every right to be there. He has a key. His sister used to be friends with someone who owned this home, and she gave him a key so he could come whenever he wanted. You proceed to inform him that the ownership has changed, and he has no right to be there. But he says he has as much right to be there as you do, and he isn't leaving. You tell him, "This is *my* home! My name is on the deed!" And he asks why, if it is your home, would you not have collected all the keys or changed the locks to keep people like him out? You explain that had you known, you would have. You had no idea the previous owners would have freely given access to their home. For a few minutes, you stand there yelling, "Get out! This is my home!" But the person doesn't budge, and although the noise causes the vermin to startle, they just move from under one piece of furniture to the next. They don't want to leave either.

The issue of who owns the house is not in question. But it's clear that there have been compromises to the security of the home; there have been too many ways in. You realize that although the house is yours, and that will not change, there is a lot of baggage you are now left to deal with—and you are somewhat powerless to handle it on your own. So, as the owner, you decide to take action. You stop yelling in the centre of your home. Instead, you exercise your authority you have over your home. You call the exterminator and get the unwanted vermin removed. You buy traps. You shut the bathroom window. You contact the authorities to remove the extra visitors. You change the locks. You remove the rental ads. You fire the person who has been "caring for" the property. You remove all places where you were once opening up your home to others and remove the means through which unwanted people and things were gaining entry, so they can't ever do so again.

It's always been your home. Possession has never been the issue. A desire to care properly for the property has never been the issue. It wasn't because you thought you had possession but didn't. It wasn't because you didn't really inherit it. It wasn't because you weren't really caring about your property. But due to circumstances within and out of your control, things took hold of your home in a way you never wanted or imagined—or even realized was possible.

That's what happens for many Christians who still feel stuck in a level of spiritual warfare that they can't get free from. We became Christians, and we are Christ's—the ownership is secure, and the inheritance we received is not something anyone or anything in the earthly or spiritual realm can take from us. But, depending on our history, depending on choices we have made, depending on sin in our lives, depending on our family history and the sin in their lives, and depending upon the consequences of all that—we may find ourselves bequeathed with more than just our heavenly home. We may have also acquired some squatters along the way that need to be removed. Telling people they didn't really become Christians doesn't help deal with squatters. Pointing the finger at someone's sinfulness doesn't help catch the vermin under the furniture. This isn't about questioning someone's sincerity about committing to Christ! It's about a spiritual battle that rages around us that we are told to be on the alert about.

Because this book is about God's love, and not about spiritual warfare, I am going to leave you to explore for yourself where to go for help in these particular situations. There are many wonderful resources written by highly qualified, credible sources that you can read to seek some answers and direction about how you too can be free. You will find a list of those resources in appendix C.

I will say that *all of God's promises about freedom and protection apply to you too.* And when Jesus said that His disciples would be able to do what He did, He wasn't meaning that for everyone except you. You have the same inheritance in Christ as everyone else—and He came to set you free too. However, there may be a level of spiritual bondage or captivity that requires a more specialized response than what I have discussed so far. We do have authority in Christ to secure our freedom—it is there for you too. Don't give up. Don't allow the enemy to discourage you and make you think you are stuck forever, that these promises don't apply to you. They do. And remember 1 Thessalonians 3:3—He *will* strengthen and protect you from the evil one. He *will.* And He will set you free—that's what He came to do (Isaiah 61:1). For everyone. Including you. Because He *so* loves you.

CHAPTER FOUR

Love Means Rest

*"Come to me, all you who are weary and burdened, and
I will give you rest."*

Matthew 11:28

Rest. Who doesn't need more of that?

I read somewhere that in order to truly recover from sleep deprivation you need to replace the sleep you have been deprived of, hour for hour. I'd be MIA for about five years if I did that! But rest is about more than sleep—it's about getting a reprieve. About taking a step back from busyness, the new normal of our society. About being refreshed and rejuvenated. About being given what you need from the only One who can give it to you.

It may seem simple, but consider it: how else would you expect to get what you need to do what He's asked except to seek it in the still and secret silence where He is?

This issue of rest is a work in progress for me. God continues to teach me about how important it is and how rest is intimately tied to His love for me. It is my prayer that what He has shown me will help you as well—because giving you rest is a real, vital way that God desires to show you His love.

Busy, Busy, Busy!

Let's start with a bit of brainstorming. You can do this in your journal or just in your head. What are some of the things that fill your life and interfere with your ability to rest? And remember, I don't just mean sleep. I can think of a few to get you started: work, housework, children, children's activities, volunteer work, yard work, friends, family obligations, church activities, studying, shopping, bill paying. Are there some I missed that you feel get in *your* way?

Deep, Soulful Places

In our society, where the goal is to be quick, efficient, effective, productive and accomplished, it is difficult to see the toxic effects on our lives. We find ourselves flitting from one demand to another, convinced that it's normal and wondering what's wrong with *us*. Why aren't we liking it? Why can't we keep up?

Why are we just plain tired?

As I've considered this state of affairs and the things that demand my time, I've realized something. When I'm out of time, two important parts of my life take the hit: me, and my relationship with God. And I need both to truly enjoy my life!

Most women have been programmed to do everything for everyone else first. This leaves us in a perpetual state of personal sacrifice. I do it at work with clients in crisis, giving up my lunch hour or forfeiting my breaks. At home, the kids need to eat three hours before my husband does, so I usually end up finishing what the kids didn't eat or nibbling what I'm preparing for the adults and then don't take a proper meal. I've cancelled my gym membership because it went unused so long, and I've missed quiet times with God because of demands screaming (sometimes literally) for my attention.

It's not like I think that I'm not valuable or worth the time or that quiet times aren't important. Because I do believe that both my quiet times and I are important. Yet it seems that things that are "just for me" often get pushed aside out of seeming necessity. I'm confident that many of you know what I'm talking about. I am busy because of my choices—church, family, full-time work, kids' sports, cleaning, cooking healthy food, friendships—all good stuff. All choices I consciously made. But all take time.

When you fly in an airplane, what do they tell you to do with those oxygen masks that pop down in case of emergency? Put on your own oxygen mask before you attempt to help someone else. Why? Because if *you* can't breathe, you won't be conscious. How are you going to help someone else if you're unconscious?

This is true in all areas of life. I'm a way better mom, friend, wife, mother, worker and human being when I'm not oxygen deficient, tired, hungry, burned out and spiritually dry because of not taking time to *rest*.

It's so simple, yet so hard.

You know the things that make you busy, that interfere with your rest. The question that really needs our attention is, why? What's the underlying reason you fly at Mach 10 daily? What are some thoughts or feelings that might compel you to overcommit, to fill your time with more than your plate can hold and to say yes when you need to say no? In your journal, beside the list of activities, write the thoughts and feelings that come to mind. Maybe you're compelled by guilt. Or responsibility. Maybe you feel you are the only one who can do it, or you just always have. Maybe you think you should because you were asked or because it's easier than saying no. Maybe it feels good to help. Or maybe you *do* enjoy it, but it's just gotten to be too much. Maybe you procrastinate or don't manage your time well. The reasons we don't rest are endless.

For many women, the inability to stop and rest is connected to *approval.* When we're seeking approval, we know we can gain it easily by doing things that earn us acclaim. Taking on more than we should can become gratifying because we know it will help someone out or make someone happy. And there's also seeking approval from God, when we believe He's pleased with us for what we do for Him. From one approval seeker to another, please hear me: God is more concerned with who you *are* than with what you *do.* The trouble is, many of us know we really *can* earn human approval based on what we do for others and God. If you're in the prison of earning your value by your own efforts, God yearns for you to stop and rest. *"Come to me,"* He says, *"...and I will give you rest"* (Matthew 11:28). He doesn't say, "Be busy for me." He says, *"Be still, and know that I am God"* (Psalm 46:10).

Some who are more comfortable with doing than being may have already thought of at least ten quotes from Scripture to support the importance of being busy for God in lieu of resting. Things like "Faith without works is dead" and "They know us by our fruit" and "Idle hands are the devil's workshop." Not to mention, He also said, "Go and do likewise." And, "Shine your light," and a million other things that have "doing something" attached to them. And then there is also the blessing we receive from Him for all we accomplish.

All of these things are true. And there's no question that God blesses when we do the work *He's* asked us to do. However, *being* has to come *before* doing. Air is needed before you breathe. Your oxygen mask before another's. There is an order. I'm not saying we shouldn't serve. I'm not saying our faith shouldn't include works. And I'm not saying we should all quit our areas of ministry for the sake of rest. Not necessarily, but maybe. Because some women searching for approval are *running from* something. And keeping busy keeps them distracted from the dark places in their lives, whether it be trauma, conflict in relationships, pain, grief, sickness, loneliness or unconfessed sin. Being busy provides a "legitimate" distraction from the hard stuff and helps them justify ignoring the internal and relational work that desperately needs attention.

For other women, it's where they get their worth. The more they are "needed," the more worth they feel. The problem is that their joy is based on not who they *are* in Christ but what they *do* for Him and others, which means they need to be continually *doing* to maintain their feeling of worth.

I've grown a lot in this area, but in my early twenties "approval seeking" was a big one for me, and it still rears its ugly head on occasion. As I examined my history in serving in the Church, for example, this was so obvious to me that it was almost comical. At the church we attended before moving and having children, at one time I was involved in seven different ministries in addition to working full time. *Seven.* I kept getting asked, and I didn't want to let anyone down. I didn't want to let God down either, for that matter. I felt that if I had a free night and they needed me, I should do it, even if that was my only free night all week. They were all good ministries, all important and all ones that I was able to offer something to, so I said yes. I also found it very hard to say no to a pastor—partly because of his position and partly because it felt like I was somehow saying no to God.

But I got to the point that I began fantasizing about having a baby to slow down (do you hear the absolute insanity of that statement?), which clued me in to the fact that something wasn't quite right. The lies of the enemy were underneath my reasons for saying yes. Things like:

* *I'd be letting God down.*
* *Taking time for myself is selfish.*
* *Saying no to the pastor is saying no to what God has shown him He wants from me.*

How much time do you think I had to spend alone with God when I was so busy serving in the church? How much refreshing rest do you think happened when I was that busy? How often do you think I was able to be still and *know* Him?

I had fallen into a trap (or seven) of the enemy designed to rob me of the *rest* of God. It was the best way to wear me down so I didn't have anything left to give. The one thing I didn't have time to do was stop. I couldn't listen to Him to see if what I was doing was what *He* wanted me to do. Pretty effective tactic, if you ask me: use the Church and my desire to serve and please God to deprive me of rest *from* God.

He wasn't asking me to fill every night of the week. He was asking me to come to Him.

To a certain extent, everything I was doing was good and came from a good motive. But I didn't realize that the approval-seeking part of me was also at work. That was not about just God's approval, but *man's.* That's where the prison bars fell down around me and I became stuck. I couldn't come *to* Him, because I was too busy doing *for* Him. Too busy to get what I desperately needed—His rest.

The great news is, when we come to Him for the rest He offers, good things happen. God's promises are to show us more of Himself and His character in a real, free relationship with Him. He's loving and cares that we get this *so* much that He gave His own Son to die in our place. That love prompts His continual care for our every need. He knows we need rest. He knows the cares of this world, the hurt and the woundedness that threaten to overtake us at times. He knows that the things we face are almost unfathomable for us and are not possible to overcome by human standards. He knows we will be stretched, tested, and maybe even persecuted. And so He says to come to Him so He can fill us up with what we truly need.

I love the picture presented to us in Isaiah 40:31 of resting in God. It says, *"But they that wait upon the LORD shall renew their strength; they shall mount up with wings as eagles; they shall run, and not be weary; and they shall walk, and not faint"* (KJV). Isn't that beautiful? When we come to Him, wait on Him, trust in Him, lay it all before Him…He will give us rest. He will give us what we need. We will be strengthened like that magnificent eagle soaring high above the clouds, needing to only spread our wings, with Him underneath us enabling us to fly. No wing flapping required. Just effortless soaring. Easy to not get tired out when you are still and someone else is keeping you up. That's what happens when what we are doing for Him comes from stopping, resting and just *being* with Him, instead of from our own need for approval, accomplishment or inability to say no. We are carried by Him and by the nourishment we get from His rest.

A relationship with Christ is not supposed to burn us out—that goes against the message of the verses we have been reflecting on. The closer we are to Him, the more refreshed and rejuvenated we will be. He says so. It's what He promises us. That's why it's so important to know if what we have committed (or over-committed) ourselves to is of Him.

Take a moment now and do a quick inventory before God. Spend some time quietly asking Him to speak to your heart, asking Him to reveal to you if you are being deceived into being busy for reasons other than obedience to Him. Reflect on those two lists you just finished making. Remember as you reflect that His promise to you, because He loves you *so* much, is that if you come to Him, He will give you rest. Not one more thing to do, not additional responsibility, not less time to be still and know Him. He promises *rest*. Ezekiel 34:15 says, *"'I will feed My flock and lead them to rest', declares the Lord GOD"* (NASB). And in that rest, He will give you the strength to handle the very thing that is making you weary. So...is it Him who is asking all this of you?

An Example for Us

Jesus modelled rest for us. He had no problem resting, being still and coming to the Father. He went away from the needy crowd to sleep in a boat (Mark 4:35–41) and was sleeping through a violent storm that the disciples feared would kill them all. He drew away from the crowd to pray (Mark 1:35; Luke 6:12). Here He is, sent to the earth to be with the people and teach them, heal them and tell them about His Father's love, and He removes Himself from that heavenly assignment to spend time in prayer. He went to His Father to be given rest. He fellowshipped in private with his closest friends (John 14:1–31), pulling away from the work that He was sent to do so that He could refuel.

As He always does, He lived out what He told us to do. If anyone has the right to feel busy, it's God! He's got the whole universe to take care of. Can you imagine the size of *that* to-do list?! And yet He values rest. He took it for Himself during the creation of the universe, on the seventh day (Genesis 2:2). He built rest into His formation of the world, and He made it part of His inspired message to us. Why? I think it's because He knows His creation. He knows what we need, how crucial rest is to life. And because He loves us *so* much, He wants to give us what we need.

Also, He is supremely wise. He knows that you have to have something in order to be able to give it to someone else, the "putting your own oxygen mask on before you try to help someone else put theirs on" premise that is explained at the beginning of every airplane flight.

He tells us to come to Him and He will give us rest. So He rests so He has it to give. He shows us what to do so that we get what we need. We could get into quite a significant theological debate about whether or not God actually *needs* to rest to be able to give us rest. Since He's God, and all powerful, does He really *need* to rest? I'm going to ask that we not get distracted from the significance of the act. Because, the bottom line is, whether He *needed* to or not, He did. And He thought it was important enough to include in the account of creation. Not only that, but the New Testament records many instances of Jesus resting. There is significance in the fact that Almighty God rested. And there is significance in the fact that He recorded it for us in His Holy Word so that we would read it and not be able to discount its significance.

Rest Isn't Just Physical

I alluded to this a bit earlier, but it is such an important part of God's demonstration of love to us, it deserves some more attention. In the Amplified Version, Jesus' words are,

> Come to Me, all you who labor and are heavy-laden and over-burdened, and I will **cause you** to rest. [I will ease and relieve and refresh your souls.] Take My yoke upon you and learn of Me, for I am gentle (meek) and humble (lowly) in heart, and you will find rest (relief and ease and refreshment and. recreation and blessed quiet) for your souls. For My yoke is wholesome (useful, good—not harsh, hard, sharp, or pressing, but comfortable, gracious, and pleasant), and My burden is light and easy to be borne. (Matthew 11:28–30, AMP, emphasis added)

It's so easy to assume that we already fully grasp what Scripture means, isn't it? And in doing so we can limit our understanding of its full meaning, its context and our ability to appreciate its inexhaustible richness. I'm pretty sure I'm not the only person who has read this passage and thought it's referring merely to a physical break. Which I do think it is, but I no longer believe that's all it means. We need more than a physical reprieve. And God promises to meet *all* our needs (Philippians 4:19). So when He says He will give us rest it must be in all areas—mind, heart and spirit as well.

Most women need rest from the cares of this world that can weigh them down like they're the family pack mule. Women in general are naturally inclined to be caregivers, to carry one another's burdens, which is biblical, but sometimes it's a very heavy load. And we get overburdened, like our passage says. We feel the weight so heavy on our shoulders, and it can really take its toll. But how do you tell someone they are becoming too much? That you don't want to carry their burden anymore? That you need a break from their pain? Most of us couldn't—wouldn't—do that. But, we need a break. *We* need to be filled up and carried for a bit.

Jesus says, come to Him and He'll give it to you. When you are worn down, overburdened, weary (as some translations put it), come to Him, and He'll give you what you need. Come to Him in prayer, alone. Come to Him with someone you trust who can seek Him with you or for you in your pain. Spend time with Him in His Word or in worship. Go away with Him alone and just be with Him in the stillness. Come to Him however suits you best. He is happy to have you come as you are. As you like.

Maybe you need a fresh perspective on the person you are helping. Maybe you need a good laugh. Maybe you need to not be the one carrying the burden anymore. He knows. So He tells us to come to Him and He will take care of us. He will give us rest. He reminds us that His expectations of us are light. He doesn't weigh us down. He lifts us up. He offers us, in Him, the break that we need.

This is important, not only because of the reprieve, but also because it ensures that we don't try to do more than is ours to do. How easy it is to get a saviour complex, to feel that if *we* aren't involved, everything will fall apart. When we are coming to Him, leaving these cares and burdens with Him, it helps us stay clear about who the ultimate helper is and what our role is in the process. And sometimes it can be the opposite. We don't want to be the only one doing the burden-carrying, but there doesn't seem to be any other takers, so we feel stuck and overwhelmed. Jesus says, "Come to Me. I'll carry that load for you, and instead, you can carry *My* load, which is light. So you can get some rest."

Sometimes, the break we need is from our *own* problems. Some seem to have been given more than their fair share of heavy loads. In those times we can feel the least loved and cared for by God. And it's in those times that the enemy tries to have a field day with our belief in God, His faithfulness to us and His care for us. When it seems to be one thing after another with no break, no reprieve and no help, the enemy attempts to convince us that we aren't important enough to be helped. That He has abandoned us. That He doesn't really love us. Or, that we deserve the relentless heartbreak and hardship we are experiencing. That God's promises don't apply to us.

This is hard. The reality is that there are no quick fixes. Drinking, drugs, sex, people, exercise, even self-care strategies, can all provide mere distractions from the problems. They don't take the problem away. Counselling helps, but it is hard work, and it doesn't give us a break from the problem itself. I'm a therapist, so I know. It *does* help, but anyone who has done healing in therapy knows it's not easy, and it doesn't give *rest* from our problems. Only God can give us a rest from our problems. Only He can provide what we need in our hearts and spirits to give us a reprieve so we can be refreshed. There is healthy self-care: things like counselling, exercise in moderation, spa services, relaxation and prayerful meditation can be helpful adjuncts to rest. His rest gives the foundation to all of these so they have His substance behind them.

He tells us that we don't need to worry, because He cares for the birds of the fields, so how much more will He care and provide for those He *so* loves (Matthew 6:26–32)? The lie of the enemy is that if we are facing some very deep waters, God is not fulfilling this promise in our lives. We tend to look to our external circumstances as an indication of whether or not He is there for us. But often when we can't see He's helping, it's because we're five steps ahead of where He wants to meet us. He often needs us to start by coming *back* to Him. So how do we do that? By *"casting all your care upon Him, for He cares for you"* (1 Peter 5:7, NKJV). It doesn't say He will remove all your problems from you. It doesn't even say He will solve them for you. It says He will care for you. Cast your problems on Him—come to Him, take His yoke instead—and He'll carry them.

He'll infuse you with what you need so that the weight doesn't burden you the way it did before. The load hasn't changed, but you no longer have to carry it. Psalm 55:22 says, *"He will sustain you; he will never let the righteous be shaken." Never.* This is the truth to defeat the enemy's lies. Yes, it is so hard right now. Yes, it feels like more than one person should have to bear. But He will not let you down. He will not let you fall. He will sustain you. And He will give you rest. Because He promises He will, and He never breaks His promises. Again, it's not that the circumstances have changed, necessarily. It's what He does for you personally in the midst of them. He gives you a reprieve from the weight of it all because of how He meets you there. And honestly, once you experience it, you realize how much *better* His rest is than the temporary reprieve that comes from all the other ways we seek to be free…like running, like working harder.

He gives you what you need to be able to cope. Sometimes, He chooses to perform a miracle, and the weight is gone. But He will always give us rest when we come to Him. In Philippians 4:13 Paul says, *"I can do all things through Christ who strengthens me"* (NKJV). The strength we need, the encouragement, the wisdom, the resilience, the support. The refuelling. Because He loves us *so* unfathomably much.

When you love someone who's down, you do whatever you can to help them. You will carry the load for them, if they will let you. You want to do whatever makes it possible for them to continue. How much more when we're talking about God and His love!

If you have never felt His rest before or you've carried more than your fair share for far too long, this may sound trite and even insensitive. The depth and breadth of some folks' pain is immense. Yet, having sat with people who have lived through some of life's worst atrocities, I've seen this truth demonstrated time and again. I've witnessed with my own eyes the weight shifting. I've also experienced it myself, in ways I did not expect or know I needed or even imagine would matter.

And it may not always be flashy, but each time it's a true miracle.

Deep, Soulful Places

Practices for Rest

My life in the past few years has become incredibly full. I don't have much downtime. I have learned from my past (seven ministries was too many!), and I've built in "practices for rest" that I know are foundational to being balanced and staying on course. I'm careful about guarding my daily devotional time. Alone time with my husband and each of my boys, family time outside of our commitments to just enjoy each other, and time off with friends and family are non-negotiables. God has given me such a full, rich life, but sometimes I'm just plain tired. I keep trusting that He will give me what I need to do what He is asking me to do (Philippians 4:13), and He does. But rest is a challenge.

In May of this past year, I was asked to speak at a woman's retreat on the subject of hearing God's voice. The preparation for that weekend was a very exciting journey with God for me. There were so many times when God would affirm things for me that He had laid on my heart to share. I was so excited about the weekend. I went to the retreat fully prepared to pour myself *out* for Him to the women at the retreat. I went with no expectations of being poured *into* whatsoever. I just wanted to do what He was asking of me and to share what I believed He had planned for those women to hear. Notice what I just said—"those women." I didn't consciously do it, but I realize in retrospect that I had neglected to consider that I was one of the women there at the retreat that God had a message for. Being the message bearer didn't preclude me, I soon found out.

As you are well aware of by now, I think it's important to take time away and let God speak. To journal what He says. To reflect on things with just Him, so that He can shine His light of truth on whatever topic is before Him. I don't ever want to come across as the authority or to get in the way of what God is saying—I prefer to share the ideas He has asked me to share and then have *God* confirm, affirm or dismiss the relevance in someone's life. This weekend was no different.

After the Saturday morning session, I gave the women the assignment of finding some time to be with just God and to listen to what it was He wanted to say to them on the weekend. To hear what message He had just for them, from Him. His love message to them. There were fun physical activities planned for the afternoon (treetop rope climbing, boating, etc.), and so I asked for them to find a way amongst all that to spend some time with Him so He could speak.

After lunch, before all these fun activities began, I decided to lie down on my bed for a bit of a rest. I was exhausted. Interestingly, about halfway to the retreat on the Friday I had come down with horrible pains in my stomach, which remained the whole weekend. So it was hard to sleep at night, and as a result I was tired. My plan was to rest on my bed until it was time to do treetop climbing (I thought I'd be the coolest mom ever when I came home and reported my accomplishment to my boys). I decided this was a good time for me to do the assignment I had given to the women. I would lie on my bed and talk with God and listen to Him and what He had to say to me. Instead, I fell asleep.

That in and of itself was a miracle, because the pains were so bad, I couldn't get comfortable. But not only did I sleep through my time with God, I missed the activities I had signed up for! I woke over two hours later, refreshed and completely taken aback that I had had such a long unintentional nap.

My sister-in-law was leading a yoga session that same afternoon. When I woke, I got ready to go down to yoga. The whole time I was getting ready, as I was walking down to the room for yoga, and even as I was getting my mat ready, I was thinking, *Wow, how bad is that? I go to my room to spend time with God and listen to what He has to tell me this weekend about my relationship with Him, and what do I do? I fall asleep! How embarrassing. Can't wait to share **that** with the women.*

I was feeling like quite a failure as my sister-in-law began the class (can you hear the whispers of the enemy? I can). She had some praise music playing and told us to just be still and be with God on the mat. What a failure I felt I was. I was in the middle of telling God how sorry I was for falling asleep on Him when He spoke to me so clearly. It wasn't audible, but it may as well have been. He interrupted my apology and said, "Come to me, all who are weary and heavy laden, and I will give you rest."

I began to cry on the mat. And the tears are flowing as I write this. In that moment, I realized that my nap *was* what God was saying to me. It was His message of love to me. He gave me rest because I needed it. I had gone to Him on that bed at the retreat, told Him I was listening and wanted to hear what He had to say…and fell asleep. The enemy had me fully onboard, believing I was "less than" spiritual for doing so. And, had I not come to Him and been back in His presence, giving Him another chance to speak with me, I might have missed His beautiful message. He knew how tired I was. He knew the physical pains I was dealing with. He knew what I needed to finish the weekend messages well. And *because He loved me,* He gave me what I needed most: rest. Reprieve. Refuelling. A message of love from Him.

I had people praying for me both at home and at the retreat. When the pains came on, I took them as an attack from the enemy, so I sought God's healing. It's hard to stand for 45 minutes and communicate effectively when the only position that offers relief is the fetal position. And remarkably, I don't remember the pains when I was speaking, just before and after. It was the rest I needed to do the work He asked of me. He didn't take the pains away completely, but He gave me rest from them. He also gave me sleep, something I so desperately needed at that particular time.

That encounter with Him on the yoga mat was powerful for me. I'm so used to being the one to meet everyone else's needs. I'm a mom and a boss, and it's just second nature. But I forget that I'm also a child, His child. And that He desires to care for me as I care for my children, if only I'd come to Him and let Him give me what I need.

I ended the Sunday session with the women spending half an hour alone with God, journaling their answers to the following questions, which I ask you to consider also:

> Who do you know God to be?
> How have you experienced Him in this way?
> How does the enemy try to prevent you from hearing God speak?
> What does He want you to know from Him?

I didn't create this exercise thinking that it was for me, but I felt God asking me to come away with Him for that half hour and leave the preparing of the last half of the session for later. So I did. And here is an excerpt of what I wrote:

> Who do I know You to be?
>
> I know You to be real. I know You to be faithful. I know You are personal. I know You care about me. I know that You are good and Your plans are good. I know that Your ultimate plan for me is that I will be more like You and I will bring You glory…
>
> You have given me strength when I didn't have any. You are good. You are my God, and I love You.
>
> The enemy tries to prevent me from hearing God in many ways: the enemy appeals to my intellect; he uses my skills as a therapist—gets me relying on me instead of God; the enemy gets me thinking about other things; he gets me focused on myself; he gets me busy; he makes me feel insecure and doubting myself and my experience.
>
> God wants me to know that He's my father—my "daddy." That He'll never leave me, even though people in my earthly

life will. That He's a big and powerful God. He wants me to know that He'll meet all my needs—even for things like sleep. He wants me to remember that I am His child –and that if I just let Him, He will meet all my needs—that even when those around me don't "worry about me"…He does. He wants me to remember that WITH HIM is the one place in all my life where I don't have to worry about taking care of someone. Where I don't have to be careful about "asking too much," relying "too much," being too needy or dependent…it is the one place of complete freedom, peace, serenity I need.

He wants me to remember how passionately He loves me. How deeply He loves me. How great He thinks I am because He's proud of His handiwork and the Son who lives in me. He wants me to never forget He will never leave me or forsake me. That He always shows up.

He gave me that love message of rest because He knew it would meet me where *my* need was that particular weekend. And He also knew it would set the stage and open the door for the other things He wanted to say to me the next day in my journaling time. I felt *so* loved as I sat there on that stump in the sun on a beautiful Sunday morning. So cherished. So important to Him. Because He knew me enough to know what I needed. Because He cared enough to give it to me. Because He wasn't content with just giving me what I needed; He made sure I knew that *He* did it, that it was from Him specifically. And then, because He *so* loves His children and wants them to feel cherished, He spoke His words of truth and care into my experience in a way I would never forget.

Because when you love someone, you want them to know it and never forget it. When you love someone, you want them to know that you don't meet their needs out of obligation or duty. You meet their needs out of love because they are that important and special to you. Jesus gave me rest. He gave me a two-hour nap. He gave me relief from the pains while I spoke. And He gave me a reprieve from the enemy attacks on my beliefs about myself and my experience—and spoke His truth into them instead. Because He *so* loves me.

He *so* loves you too. He wants you to feel cherished. He wants to give you a love message that meets you where you are. Maybe you don't need a nap.

The specifics of my example were just for me. But I shared them so you could see that when you are *so* loved by our God, He will make sure His love message to you is specific. It won't be like mine unless you need what I needed.

Go to Him, all you who are weary. All women who need some kind of reprieve, refuelling or restoration. Go to Him. He will give you rest. You are His child. He is your Father. He will meet you where you are, He will trade your load for His, and He will fill His load for you to carry with all that you need from Him to keep going. Because He cares for you.

CHAPTER FIVE

Love Means We Have Worth

"For I know the plans I have for you" declares the
LORD, *"plans to prosper you and not to harm you,
plans to give you hope and a future."*

Jeremiah 29:11

A woman's understanding of her true worth is a passion of mine. I have been speaking about it for years, and I think there are three main reasons for this passion. The first is professional. Since I became a therapist in 1996, I have seen over and over again the vast impact that feelings of worth (or the lack thereof) have on an individual's resiliency and ability to heal, resolve conflicts and fully embrace life. Regardless of what issue causes someone to seek counselling, helping to rebuild a foundation of worth is very often the starting place in therapy…because without it, it is very hard to get unstuck and move forward therapeutically.

The second is personal. I have been on my own journey in understanding my worth, where it lies and what it really means. And I have witnessed many friends and family members on their journeys of finding self-worth. I have seen its importance firsthand. And, although I'm sure there will always be new truths that God can reveal to me about this, I can certainly testify to the freedom it offers, and I want the same for you.

The third reason for my passion is spiritual. Women's lack of understanding of their worth is one of the most powerful areas Satan uses to keep us from being all that God intended us to be, because he knows full well that a woman in touch with her worth in Christ is a powerful weapon for the kingdom of God and a tremendous threat to the kingdom of darkness.

God created each of us the way we are for a reason. He does not make any mistakes. There is purpose behind our design and inherent worth in it as a result. Despite what the enemy tries to do, God is in the business of taking the broken and making it new. And when we are willing to accept that He created us with worth and we believe that God can use us for His purposes to bring Him glory, He will. I believe that a woman's worth is tied directly to how loved she is, and we are *so* loved. That's what makes us so dangerous. When a woman understands that she is *so* loved, she is then able to know where her worth lies. And this is the foundation on which she needs to stand as she steps out in obedience to use the gifts God designed and placed uniquely in her.

Women are bombarded daily with false messages. We hear, see, and are even told that our appearance is paramount, our careers define us and our wealth enhances us. These are not loving messages. They don't make us *feel* like we are on a solid, strong foundation. They usually make us feel insecure, self-conscious and off-kilter. And when we are in that place, we end up immobilized and unable to see, hear and feel His purposes for us. When God created us, as it says in Jeremiah 29, He had a plan. And it was to give us a hope and a future. And yet, I know that for many women, their inability to grasp that they have worth, and *why* they have worth, means that believing there is hope and a future is a big stretch.

It's very easy to get swayed by the messages the enemy has intentionally designed to work against us as we seek to understand our worth. Satan uses the means he finds most effective. Often what makes it effective is that we don't realize Satan is at work, because what we are dealing with just seems a part of everyday life, not something purposefully designed to undermine our confidence in who God made us to be and why He made us that way.

In my teen years, I used to measure my worth by the size of my thighs. You snicker, but it's true. I was *so* distracted by them—to the point that what I would wear, where I would sit, how I would sit, what I would eat and what I would do were all determined by my thighs and how wide they would spread when I sat down. I couldn't wait for the preacher to tell us to open up our Bibles at church, because I had a large NASB study Bible, and it would completely cover my legs when it was open. It would allow me to stop obsessing about how fat my legs looked spread across the seat and actually listen to the speaker. The Bible was definitely my shield…but not in the way those verses mean. Of course I realize now that I had a distorted view of my body, much like you see reflected back to you in a house of mirrors at a community fair. In my mind, my thighs were massive.

You might be wondering what would cause me to be so down on my appearance. Did something happen to me that made me feel badly about myself in my own skin? I wish I could say yes to you, because it would make my struggle seem so much more rational and logical, but I can't. I had a family that was very complimentary. No one violated my body to make me not like it. But there certainly were lots of messages in society about how young girls should look, and having curves was definitely not one of them—well, not curves *below* the waist anyway! Add that when I was young I had subconsciously decided that the best way to keep "control" over things in my life was to be as perfect as I could. *Don't make people mad. Don't disappoint them. Please them. Help them. Blend in. Make them happy. Wherever possible, be the best you can—or the best, period. It gives you a buffer. It helps make others happy. And it feels good.* I had not realized it, but I had bought into the lie that external "perfection" brings happiness. But when that lie is being whispered, the part that always gets left out is "It's not possible." I kept falling short—more specifically, my thighs kept falling short. And therefore I was trapped in this perpetual feeling of "not good enough."

It wasn't until my late teens or early twenties that I realized what was going on and began to reject the lies and embrace the truth. What freedom that brought me! I can honestly say that although I'm not a big fan of my thighs to this day, they no longer define me or determine my worth. And now, when they spread out on the chair when I sit, I don't immediately begin thinking about what I can do to fix that or hide it. In fact, it is rare that I actually take the time to notice anymore…because I know now, that's not what really matters about me.

The Bible Is a Love Story

The Bible is very clear about the fact that we, as God's beautiful creation, have worth. God's countless actions and statements recorded in Scripture demonstrate that we mean everything to Him. He is constantly proving He loves us.

One of my favourite passages that speaks powerfully of this is found in John 8. Jesus was teaching in the temple when Pharisees and other teachers of religious law dragged a woman in front of Him and announced to Him and all who were there listening that she had just been caught in the act of adultery. Can you imagine the humiliation she would be facing? Not only did they actually catch her in the act, they dragged her in front of a crowd and announced it publically. (I'm so thankful that all my sins don't get announced that way.) According to the religious laws of that day, she was to be stoned for her actions. These religious leaders were very interested in finding a way to trap Jesus and destroy His credibility with the people. They didn't like that He was getting all the attention. I suspect they really didn't care about the woman and her actions—she was just a pawn. But Jesus cared. He loved her. He knew what they were doing, that they were trying to trip Him up. But someone He loved was in trouble, so that was where He focused.

He didn't engage in a discussion with the religious leaders. He didn't quote the law to prove He knew what was written. He didn't even speak to them, He just wrote in the dust with His finger. He wasn't about to give these men the satisfaction of destroying the life of someone He loved, just to make a point. Instead, He came to her defense. Isn't that what we all crave? Someone who loves us enough to stand up for us against our accusers. Someone who will not be swayed by the stories (or truth) others tell about us. Someone who puts their own reputation on the line to stand with us in the midst of the mess that is our life.

Jesus didn't say what she did was right. Because it wasn't. And He is truth. But He also didn't act like she was somehow worse than anyone else because she had gotten caught in her sin. (I always wonder, where was the man...the other half of the act of adultery?) But He still defended *her*. Not her behaviour; her. He acknowledged the reality of the situation and then said that whoever in the crowd *wasn't* guilty of something should throw the first stone at her. The passage says that the accusers began to slip away, one by one, starting with the oldest, until only Jesus, the woman and the crowd He was teaching were left. Then He asked her, *"Where are your accusers? Didn't even one of them condemn you?"* *"No, Lord,"* she answered, and He said, *"Neither do I. Go and sin no mor*e" (John 8:10–11, NLT). That's love. Protection, defense, accountability and a second chance.

That woman was loved by Him. She was *worth something* to Him. Not because of her behaviour, her looks or her status, but because He made her. If you feel unlovable, not good enough, too tainted by something or someone in your past or present, Jesus isn't going to throw any stones at you. Just by virtue of being you, you matter to Him.

What are we worth to God? Jeremiah 31:3 says, *"I have loved you with an everlasting love."* His love for us will never change. His love gives us special status in this world. It makes us His children. That fact gets thrown around so much in Sunday school and church sermons, I think its significance can get lost. But God doesn't want us to miss it. First John 3:1 says, *"See how great a love the Father has bestowed on us, that we would be called children of God; and such we are"* (NASB). We are His children, His family. We have a place with Him and an inheritance with Him, all of the things you get from a healthy earthly family, but more, because only in His family do we find our true worth. We truly have it all with Him. Being loved as one of His children is unmistakable evidence of our worth because of the significance of being *His* child. Ask any parent and he or she will testify to the strong emotion attached to that possessive love.

If you aren't a parent, don't lose the significance here. Think about people who are foster parents. They think that kids they don't even know deserve a chance to be in a loving environment. But something compels people to go a step further and actually adopt a child. There is significance in being able to say this child is "*my*" child. That permanent identification and implication of belonging is powerful for both the parents and the child. The child, being unquestionably special to those parents, becomes galvanized by the fact that they chose to adopt.

That security for the child gives a sense of permanence nothing can take away, because adoption is legal and binding. Being a child of God and loved by Him gives us worth because we have security, significance and belonging in relationship with an Almighty, perfect God. We're given a title that makes us part of a royal family, and *nothing* can change it, not our looks, not our performance, not our behaviour, not our relationships. The Bible says in Romans that *nothing* can separate us from the love of God in Christ Jesus...*nothing.*

We also have worth because we were created in His image. Genesis 1:27 says, "*So God created mankind in his own image, in the image of God he created them; male and female he created them.*" We are "image bearers" of God to the world. Our inheritance as humans and the fact that we were created in His image are keys to where our worth lies.

Remember Rose in the movie *Titanic?* She and her mother came from "old money," and in the movie, Rose's mom looked down her nose at another passenger whose money was "new." In wealthy circles, status is attached to family money— an inheritance that has been passed on through generations. Like an antique, the longer it has existed, the greater its value. This is like our spiritual heritage as well. Our worth in our family started with Adam and Eve, made in His image, and that inheritance and worth has passed from generation to generation.

God already *so* loved us the moment He created us, and He was so pleased. In Genesis 1:31 the Bible records, "*God saw all that he had made, and it was very good.*" When you look through the creation account, you can see that after God surveyed what He had created on each day, He pronounced it good. After He had made man and woman, He said it was "very good." Something set us apart from His assessment of the water, land and animal kingdom. Sometimes it's easier to see the beauty in nature and appreciate the wonder and the uniqueness of animals, birds and fish than to appreciate the beauty and worth He created in you. A beauty and worth that set you apart, higher than that of nature and the animal kingdom in His estimation, one that made Him love you the moment He created you, one that made Him call you "very good."

Deep, Soulful Places

In our materialistic society, we all know that the more valuable something seems, the more it costs. And as we established at the beginning of this journey, the highest price you can pay for something is your life. We all have worth because of the price that was paid for us, paid because of how loved we are by Him.

The fact is that Jesus died for us. God sending His Son, Jesus Christ, to die on the cross speaks powerfully to our worth because of the price that was paid to keep us. Remember my friend's email that I shared with you, when we were talking about how amazing God's love is? She was finally able to accept her worth when she realized how much God paid for her. Her eyes were opened when she made the connection between the price that was paid for her and her worth in God's eyes.

His Plans for a Future for Us

God knew we would need more than just some food, water, shelter and companionship. He knew He was creating us in His image, and so there would be much more to the story. He knew the depth we could go in our thinking, our understanding of life and our definition of self. He knew that central to our feelings of worth and value would be the fact that we would need to have purpose here on this earth, beyond just existing. It is such a powerful demonstration of our ultimate worth in Him that He clearly states that He has a plan to give us a future.

We spend our entire lives working towards our futures. When we go through elementary school, we are taught what we need to know so that we have the skills we need to build on for future education and ultimately life. We begin talking about what we want to be "when we grow up." When we enter high school, we are expected to take courses that prepare us for college or university or that equip us with the skills and tools to begin working in a trade. Then, once we have moved out of the schooling phase of life and we have supposedly grown up, we begin looking at what we need to do to make sure that we can live the next few decades in the lifestyle we want. So we make choices and sacrifices to plan for that. The whole time, we're hearing about how important it is to begin saving now for retirement. Hearing how unexpectedly something can happen and why we should get life and disability insurance. Why it is better to pay for our funeral now so that our family doesn't have to. Why we need both a living will and a will for after we die. We are always thinking ahead.

I'm all for planning and being prepared. My point is that this idea of a future is something we have a need to understand, engage in and plan for from the time we are little. And even those completely oblivious to God are actively engaged in striving to meet this need that He placed within us. *Or* they are not. And I would humbly suggest that when people are not actively engaged in their future (which inevitably means they are not actively engaged in their present), it is not a good thing.

One of the most depressing and dehumanizing things you can encounter is being robbed of your future. Loss of a job. Loss of a home. Loss of a person. Loss of an opportunity for advancement. Loss of confidence, which leads to loss of initiative, which leads to loss of motivation. People who don't know what they will do with their lives or don't believe they can do anything or, worse, think they can't do anything with their lives are very, very unhappy.

That is not God's plan for us. He wants to make sure we have everything we need. Including a future. He knows how important it is that we feel we have capacity to make a difference, to contribute to this world, to life. He knows that people need to use their abilities to feel there is something of worth about them that is irreplaceable.

God made you the way you are for a reason. You have capacity, competency and opportunity just because you are you. Because He chose to make you that way. That's the bottom line. That is at the crux of all this. That when God created you, in His image, in a way that made Him say "This is very good," *He had a plan for you.* His plan was that He would use you and enable you, despite all of your perceived weaknesses, hardships and trials, to make a mark on this world and in the lives of His creation *in a way only you can.* And that purpose was of such importance and you were of such value to Him that He sent His Son to die for you so that your freedom would be secured and you would have everything you need to live free, as He intended from the beginning of time.

Do not let Satan convince you that you aren't good enough, smart enough, whole enough, healthy enough, talented enough or godly enough to be used for God's kingdom. Those are just lies. Satan wants you stuck *because* God wants you free.

The Bible is full of stories about people who sinned, doubted God, or were sick, scared and hurting, and they were still used by God to fulfill His purpose. The only thing they needed to do was step out in faith and be obedient to God's call on their lives. David was considered to be a man after God's own heart, despite his sins with Bathsheba and against Uriah. Moses was used by God to set His people free, despite the fact that Moses didn't think he was a good speaker. Rahab was instrumental in helping the Israelite spies escape despite being a prostitute.

These people were not perfect, just willing to be used by God in the way He asked of them. If they had focused on what they thought made them not good enough, those amazing things would not have taken place. They didn't get perfect first and then obedient. They were just obedient despite their imperfections, and God blessed them as a result. Which makes you *feel* pretty much as close to perfect as you can get.

There is no one else in this world like you, and that was by divine design. His intention was that you, and not someone else, would do what He has for you and be what He has called you to be.

How is God calling you to make a difference in His world? I know with complete assurance that you have been created exactly the way you are for a reason. You have gifts and talents divinely ordained to make a difference for eternity. You have worth and value far above anything this world could ever offer, and that worth is secure and untouchable because of Christ's death and resurrection. You are a child of God and a beautiful image of Him. You have the means to touch this world one act at a time—just like Moses, David, Rahab and all those other biblical characters did—for the kingdom of God.

His plan is to allow us to understand how deeply we are loved and just how much worth that naturally infers on us as a result.

Hope

It is hard to talk about how God has a plan for our future without mentioning hope. Because really, they are completely entwined. You actually can't even think about a future if you don't have hope, can you?

Hope is *so* powerful. Even without God, hope is powerful. We see this truth lived out in people's actions all the time. Why do people buy lottery tickets? Hope. Why do people try new treatments for what ails them? Hope. Why do people get second and third opinions? Hope really, really matters. In counselling, as soon as we can find what ignites or sustains a person's hope, we are on our way to healing in a therapeutic context. And not surprisingly, what is intrinsically tied to a sense of hope is people's ability to see that they have worth. That they matter. That there is a point to life and, more specifically, a point to *their* lives.

God knows that. Which is why His plan for us is that we have hope. That we know that we matter. That we get that there is a reason for our existence, and that we can look to the future with positive expectation, with hope. The hope we have from God isn't tied to our circumstances. It is tied to Him. This is where we often get mixed up. We focus, and Satan encourages us to focus, on our hard experiences, the circumstances around us. And based on that stuff he asks, "Where is your hope now?" I have found that he is quite good at this. We are pretty skilled at evaluating our hope for our future based on what we see happening around us. And then we are extra good (with some expert enemy coaching) at getting stuck when it isn't what we feel we deserve.

If you don't feel that He has met your needs, I truly understand why it seems that way. You may have a need right now that is unmet, that is very valid and real. Like for food or shelter. There is hope for you too. We have every right to hope in God. Every right to trust Him to meet our needs. Philippians 4:19 says, *"And my God will meet all your needs according to the riches of his glory in Christ Jesus."* We can hang our hats on that. It is there that we get our hope, in the fact that He will meet all our needs. *He* is our hope. This relates to *all* our needs. That is what the verse says. He has the capacity to answer prayer. He knows what we need, and He has the ability to ensure that in some way, some-how, we get our needs met.

Let's start with our practical, earthly needs. Matthew 6:26 says, *"Look at the birds of the air; they do not sow or reap or store away in barns, and yet your heavenly Father feeds them. Are you not much more valuable than they?"* Yes, you are. *Much* more valuable. You, in comparison, are "very good." I say this with great respect, knowing there are some who struggle for every basic need to be met. As a result, you may not like my comments about this. But I believe that God is very creative and varied in how He meets these needs. And, at times, His definition of need is very different than ours. Far be it from me to suppose that I know the mind of God. I know only what the Bible tells me about His heart. It says He will meet all our needs and we are more valuable than the birds. I trust that is truth.

Often, *we* determine our needs and how we think they should be met. When things don't pan out, we think God hasn't shown up for us. When we need food, if we can't go buy it ourselves, we think He isn't meeting our need for food. Is temporary dependence on a friend or neighbour, the food bank or soup kitchen *how* we want our need to be met? No, and I don't blame anyone for feeling that way. But until God works His plan out, that just may be how He is meeting the need. That is such a harsh truth to speak. I don't understand why some people seem to get their needs met so effortlessly and respond so ungratefully and why others have to struggle. That is something I hope to ask Him about in heaven one day. I do know, however, that He is faithful, and He will meet our needs. Even though it may not be how we want them met.

Deep, Soulful Places

Years ago, I heard a story you may have heard too. There was once a town that got flooded. The waters were so high, everyone climbed to the rooftops to escape the water. One of the men was a faithful servant of God who believed in the power of prayer, so as he climbed to his roof he prayed, "God, I believe You take care of Your children, so I ask that You rescue me from this danger. I know You will answer my prayer, because You are powerful and You answer Your children when they call on You."

Shortly thereafter, a helicopter flew by with a rope ladder. Someone yelled, "Grab on—we will take you to safety!" But the man waved them away. "No thank you. God is going to rescue me!" A neighbour cruised by in his motorboat. "Come on!" "No thank you," the man said. "God is going to save me!" The water swirled higher as a woman in a canoe paddled up, asking the man to climb aboard. Again, he waved her on.

Suddenly, a large wave swept through the town, and the man was lost. When he stood before God, he was confused. "Don't get me wrong, Father. I'm glad to be here in heaven with you. But I trusted you to save me, and yet I died. Why?"

"My precious child," God said. "You had every reason to trust me, and I did try to save you. I sent you a helicopter, a motorboat and a canoe. What did you expect?"

Sometimes we can be so focused on our needs being met a certain way, we miss they are still being met—by Him—just maybe not how we might want. I know I have overlooked some helicopters in my day. I have turned my nose up at a few motorboats over the years. And I certainly wasn't thrilled to see some of the canoes that have passed by my rooftop.

We sometimes have open sharing times at church, and during one such sharing time a woman stood and talked about how amazing God was and how He took such good care of her. We attend a church in the centre of an affluent area, so it's easy to make assumptions about people's lifestyles based on where the church is. She talked about His faithfulness and goodness, about how loved she felt. And then she said why. She had been homeless twice in the past year. And when she called out to God, He answered. Her daughter ran away, and she feared for her safety. But she had hope in God and His promises to her, and her daughter came home. She chose to reach out and ask her church community for help. They responded, and her needs were met. It is so easy to get focused on our circumstances and whether or not we therefore have hope. Her circumstances didn't cause her to lose her hope in Him; they caused her to look *to Him* with hope.

I remember a woman I counselled years ago. She didn't have two nickels to rub together. She had a roof over her head, but she had four kids and often didn't know where their next meal would come from. But she hoped in God. And He always provided. One day, at Christmastime, she was given a turkey. A turkey is a great way to feed a lot of people for a few days, so she saw it as God's provision for her, something she could not have afforded on her own. However, she heard of someone worse off than her, and she decided they needed the turkey more than her. I confess, I was shaking my head at her, thinking she was giving away what God had given to take care of her. Silly me. Because when she woke up the next day, she found a different turkey on her porch, put there by some anonymous person. He met her need for food, and through meeting her need He met someone else's too. Because she hoped in Him. Because she had her eyes fixed on Him.

Her circumstances stayed pretty rotten and discouraging for many years. There were times where a meal was a need. But He provided. Her hope was in Him for the earthly stuff. But because He met her earthly needs, deep spiritual needs were met as well. She felt valuable to God—she became aware of how much He loved her and how much worth she had in His eyes because He continued to provide for her, time and time again. She didn't get a token turkey from Him and then see Him move on to the next person. No, He loved her. She mattered to Him and to this world. Her family had to wear hand-me-downs, which wasn't their choice. They had to accept the generosity of strangers, which hurt their pride at times. And they had to ask for help as well, which wasn't fun. But He always took care of them. And because their eyes were on Him, they had hope in Him.

I'm reminded of the time when Jesus was walking on the water in the midst of a terrible storm (Matthew 14). He was on the mountainside praying, and the disciples were in the boat. The storm came up, and things got really scary for those in the boat. Jesus knew they were scared, so He went out to them. He walked to them on top of the swirling, angry waves. They actually thought He was a ghost at first, until He got closer. Peter was so relieved to see Him, he hopped out of the boat and started walking towards Him on the water. Don't you just love Peter? He makes me know Jesus is okay with us being human. Peter was emotional, he could be impulsive, and he sometimes spoke before he thought. Yet Jesus picked him as one of His most important disciples and loved him.

It was all going miraculously well, until Peter took his eyes off Jesus and looked down at the water swirling around him. As soon as he did that, he began to sink. But his need was to live and not drown, so Jesus saved him. And then Jesus calmed the storm.

That's the spiritual hope we have. Jesus didn't prevent the storm from happening. Nor did He prevent Peter from fixating on the swirling waters. But Jesus did meet Peter where he was and offered him help, comfort and His presence in the midst of it all. That is how Jesus meets our spiritual needs. We will have Him with us, leading us, guiding us, helping us in the midst of it all. That's hope. Although the water is swirling below us, He will not let us drown.

We also have future hope that one day, when this world is done, we will get to be with Him forever in heaven. That we will no longer be stuck in the pain and hardship of a fallen world, but that because we are His children we're in line for our inheritance in Him, and we'll one day spend eternity in heaven with Him. There is nowhere in the Bible that promises that being a child of God will protect us from the fallen world we live in. Just that He will be with us in it and that at the end of our lives we will get to be in heaven with Him forever, which *is* perfect, protected, pure, abundant and altogether lovely.

And the spiritual dimension of hope, rooted in His presence and His eternal promise, offers us earthly hope because it offers protection from the heaviness of life. It guards and protects our hearts and minds in Christ Jesus (Philippians 4:7) and helps us not get mired down by what's around us. It offers us something to focus on that keeps our attention off the swirling waters. Not that they aren't there. Not that they don't cause fear or worry at times. We are human. Just that His presence and His promise offer a buffer. Offer us something in that deep, soulful place only He can touch, which otherwise remains empty and longing for Him.

Like it says in Romans 15:13, "*May the God of hope fill you with all joy and peace as you trust in him, so that you may overflow with hope by the power of the Holy Spirit.*" He is the God of hope. And His hope fills us with joy and peace (despite our circumstances) when we trust Him—for both the temporal and the spiritual, which in turn helps us have more hope!

The hard things of life are real. And some people do have it worse than others. That's not our fault. It's not. Those are lies from the enemy designed to rob us of the hope that's rightfully ours in Christ Jesus through the Holy Spirit. Those lies tempt you to throw in the towel and decide there's no point hoping in Him. Don't be distracted from the truth. You have worth. You matter to Him.

Why does Satan go to such trouble to interfere with our understanding of our worth in this world? He must be more aware of our worth than many of us are. He must get what God intended for our lives more than some of us do. Personalize that for a second. He must be keenly aware of just how dangerous you are when you're fully cognizant of what you have to offer to this world. You, filled with hope, must be very, very dangerous.

Our worth, value, purpose, meaning and place in Christ and in this world is so secure, so valuable and so precious that Satan wants and *needs* to do something to get our focus off that. And that is because if our focus is on who we are in Christ through His death and resurrection, that is where we get the anchor for our worth. The storm can rage around us, but our understanding of our worth is secure, fastened to an immovable safety. We are on solid ground. And solid ground enables us to move forward. To act. To live. To really live.

The enemy's purpose is to steal, kill and destroy (John 10:10). So us really living is a threat to him.

Choosing to Ignore the Lies—The Real Challenge

As I've contemplated who God is and what His Word says, I am unable to ignore that some of the frustrating traditional church responses often given to those in pain are built on biblical truths that cannot be discounted. I know how many different needs, wounds and rotten experiences many have endured. I never want to sound like I'm glossing over that. I have journeyed with far too many people to even consider being disrespectful of that pain. However, the fact is, when we're focused on Him and put our hope in Him, not only will He answer, but we *will* get spiritual and deep *help* from Him available nowhere else.

We can trust that because we matter and are worth everything to Him, He has a plan for us, and He will ensure that we have what we need to carry that purpose out. When we stop listening to the lies about us and our worth, we are able to see that He has an open door to what we need.

That's what Paul means in Philippians 4:13 when he says, "*I can do all things through Christ who strengthens me*" (NKJV). We don't get superpowers to do anything, which is often what we think about ourselves. We think we should be able to do it all and then get down when we can't. Can you hear the lie? No, it means if He is asking something of us, we can be assured that we already have what we need; we have how He made us, and we have Him helping, leading and guiding us.

Because we are His creation, because we are His children, because He divinely ordained our place in His world, I want to ask you the following (and perhaps you could write your answers in that journal): What is the plan and purpose He has for you? How has He made you to make a mark on His world? Do you hear Him whispering these truths about you and your worth into your ear?

Do you hear Him telling you how much He loves you? How worthwhile you are? That your presence on His earth matters to Him and matters to the world He made for you to be a part of?

Or do you hear lies? Do you hear only bad things? If you are wrestling with the lies of the enemy, let me repeat something I said earlier. Tell Satan to be quiet in Jesus' name. Then read these words *out loud*. They are the truth you have the power to believe from this moment forward:

> God made me. He made me in His image. As soon as He made me, He loved me. Enough to send His Son to die for me, save me and ensure my inheritance and my freedom for all eternity. All of this means I am worth great value in God's eyes, and in His world. How He created me, with my gifts, talents and abilities, was for a reason. I have worth just because I'm me. Because He chose to make me this way.
>
> God has a plan for me. He wants to use me and enable me, despite all my perceived weaknesses, hardships and trials, to make a mark on this world and in the lives of His creation in a way only I can. I will not let Satan convince me I am not good enough, smart enough, whole enough, healthy enough, talented enough, or godly enough to be used for God's kingdom. Because I am. That is the truth about me I chose to believe.

Don't ever forget that. Don't let the water swirling below you convince you otherwise. See Him. Hear Him. *That* is where your worth lies. He is where you will find your future and your hope.

CHAPTER SIX

Love Means He Speaks to Us

Draw near to God and He will draw near to you.

James 4:8 (NKJV)

As a counsellor, things like effective communication, resolving conflict with words and not violence, and affirming others' feelings are really important to me. I know God has a sense of humour, because He gave me two boys that have challenged my hard-core stance on all of these beliefs, and then some!

My boys are physical. Apparently, just because *I* believe you can and should talk everything out doesn't mean it naturally filters down to my boys…despite my best efforts. One of the things we have tried to teach our boys is that while you are well within your rights to defend yourself physically if someone is being physical with you, you should never be the first to be physical. Unless it is clear that you will get hurt, you should try to use your words first.

My younger son, Caleb, caught wind of an older kid "bugging" his older brother, Ethan, in the schoolyard. This boy was two to three years Caleb's senior. He was bugging Ethan like a fly bugs an elephant, but Caleb would not stand for someone messing with his brother (interestingly, *Caleb* has no problem messing with his brother). So Ethan came home from school one day reporting that Caleb had taken out this pest on the schoolyard. *He threw him down to the ground.*

I was flabbergasted! There is a zero tolerance policy at the school, so my first question was "Did a teacher see you?" (Great parenting moment, huh? Did you get caught?!). Thankfully, no teachers saw. My second question was "Caleb, what have I taught you about using your words first, before you use your hands?"

Caleb looked at me with his big blue eyes and answered "I did, Mom! I told him, 'I'm going to beat you up'—and then I did." Sigh.

Using our words matters—not just before we get physical with a bully on the schoolyard, and not just because I am a social worker. We need to speak and be spoken to so that we can understand and be understood. Engaging in ongoing, active, mutual communication draws us into a relationship. It is that reciprocity that deepens the connection and enhances the intimacy.

Have you ever been given the silent treatment by someone you were in a relationship with? It is torture! And it feels very disrespectful. It certainly does little to enhance a feeling of connectedness and intimacy. And if the silence continues, the relationship falls apart. As humans, we need communication to thrive. We can't achieve intimacy without it. Which is why God loving us means that He speaks with us.

Intimacy Requires Communication

I believe God had me wait until chapter 6 to discuss this with you because He knows us so well. I didn't plan for it. He knows the doubts we face, the hurts that cloud our vision. He knows how easy it is to put a book down and never pick it up again because we find ourselves faced with something we don't want to face. And He knows how hard the enemy works to tear down what He has built or is trying to build in our lives.

A firm foundation and a solid understanding of Him and His intentions for us are vital prerequisites for discussing these specific truths about intimacy with Him. He knew we needed to first be clear about His love, the fact that there is no condemnation, that we can be free, that He meets our needs and gives us rest and immense worth. It's the solid ground on which to examine this concept of mutual, intimate communication with Him.

And of course, it is all because He *so* loves us.

You already know that one of the most foundational tenets of a healthy, intimate relationship is good communication. Any relationship—with a family member, spouse, friend, co-worker, neighbour, or customer—requires communication to be even the least bit effective. God made it this way. And so He offers us a real relationship with Him, not some abstract, fabricated illusion. He communicates *with us*. It's not a one-way street.

God is not a silent observer. He's not concerned with formality and structure; He is concerned with us. He understands better than anyone else what we truly need, and so He desires to speak to us—to communicate with us so that we can really know Him and understand who it is that we have committed our lives to. And He isn't keeping track of how many times we talk with

Him. He speaks to us because He loves us. Have you noticed how He is pursuing intimacy with you, how He is being intentional about showing you His love in your everyday life? Like when you read something and it touches the exact place you needed touching. Or when a friend calls just when you need a word of encouragement. Or when you listen to a song and the words sound like they were written from Him to you.

Communication with God has the potential to be a very complicated topic and has been the focus of thousands of books over the years. I won't try to do it justice here; rather, I want to share just a few key thoughts on the topic: that He does speak to us and that we can hear Him and know Him intimately, personally, and have communicative reciprocal *closeness* with Love Himself, the Almighty God of the universe.

Communication with God happens. It is real. He is the same God yesterday, today and forever, which means that the same God who told Noah to build an ark is the One who speaks to you and me. It means that because He wants to reveal Himself, we don't have to feel alone or disconnected from Him. And I know that *real* communication with Him takes a relationship that feels vague and distant and makes it feel real, relevant and personal.

Students of communication will tell you there are two roles: the listener and the speaker. There are also two types of communication: verbal and non-verbal. And often the listeners will infer meaning from the speakers' non-verbal communication based on their knowledge of the speakers. Those people you know well are easier to "get," even without great verbal expression, because you know their cues and you know their history, their value set and their belief system. The same holds true with God. The better we know Him, the better we can hear what He is saying. Practice at listening to and knowledge of who is speaking to us makes all the difference.

Despite common misconceptions, God is not hard to get to know. We can't fully understand all His ways—He is God, beyond our full comprehension. However, He makes Himself quite known to anyone who wants to know Him. In fact, His intention is that every single person in a relationship with Him understands His character, His promises and His intentions for His children. He reveals himself in His Word (the Bible), His past actions, what we witness in others' lives, and our own relationship with Him. And I believe that He wants nothing more than to meet each of us in those deep, soulful places personally so that we are forever changed. So that we can stop striving for fulfillment, because we have found it in Him.

But to stop missing out, we can no longer put Him in a box. We must stop predetermining how and when He speaks and take the time to get to know Him, be alone with Him, and not focus exclusively on His holiness and greatness such that we miss His intimate desire for us.

Getting to Know Him More

The Bible is one way that God speaks to us—it's the most widely accepted, least controversial mode of communication that He uses. It is His inspired message to us, full of rich descriptions of Him and His desires for our relationship with Him. In appendix D, I have written out a list of verses that are practical descriptions He gives to help us know Him and understand Him and His heart. These messages from Him remind us that He knows us so intimately, He knows things like when we will sit or stand, lie down or get up, and He knows our thoughts (Psalm 139). They are promises of such an intimate connection to us that He will hold us up when we need it (Isaiah 41:10) and faithfully meet all our needs (Philippians 4:19). I encourage you to read the verses for yourself and let His truth wash over you. Those truths are the foundation for this discussion.

Who are we in this relationship with? Who is speaking to us? Someone who is faithful. Someone who wants the best for us. Someone we can trust. Someone who knows what we need and will make Himself known to us for our sakes.

Which means, time spent together is crucial. If we want to experience true intimacy with God, we can't expect to get there if we never take the time to be with Him. He is not going to force Himself on us. He won't corner us and demand time. That would crush intimacy. But He is there, and He is very much wanting to be with us. And when we choose to be with Him, He will meet us there, and the impact will be powerful, deep and soul quenching.

I know many people who talk about feeling distant from God, and they are mad at Him for that. They feel abandoned and alone. But when they examine their relationship with Him, they find themselves keenly aware that there hasn't been any time spent nurturing or engaging in the relationship. I remember a poster my childhood best friend had on her wall in her bedroom. It read, "If God feels far away, guess who moved?" That pretty much sums it up.

We need to shine a light on the lies of the enemy: that a lack of intimacy is because God doesn't really care as much about you as others; that you are not as important to Him as others; that He is unavailable; that you are too sinful; that it is not possible to feel close to Him because He is holy and you are not; that it is a one-sided relationship, not a real and personal one. Lies, lies, lies.

The *truth* is, *"Draw near to God and He will draw near to you"* (James 4:8 NKJV). Doesn't that sound like true intimacy? One person acts; the other responds. One person initiates; the other reciprocates. He made a way for us to have the most amazing, satisfying, intimate, life-changing relationship ever. He initiated that process. We respond to Him by accepting it, and then He promises to meet us where we are in our relationship with Him, to respond to us and interact with us in a real and personal way. All we have to do is come near to Him, and He will respond. No hoops to jump through. No perfection required. This is a real relationship we are talking about—it is a living entity, growing, changing and maturing with every single experience we choose to have with Him.

So, choose those experiences with Him. Spend time with Him, not just during set-aside times with Him. We have the opportunity to encounter Him every second of every day. For real. Because He is all knowing, all powerful, and ever present. We can make our relationship with Him an everyday, every moment, every breath experience. Think of how close you can get with someone who literally never leaves you. And who is perfect, so He will never get on your nerves!

I leave that to you to sort out, between you and Him. Because, like human relationships, every person's relationship with Him is unique. As long as the intimacy is growing and deepening, that is all that counts. What I will say, though, is that God is not bound to just our quiet time with Him to speak to us and reveal Himself to us. If we want to hear Him, God will speak to us anywhere. I do some of my best thinking and hear some of my most important messages from God while I'm drying my hair. It's true! It's a time in my day where I can't hear anything else! Another time is when I'm alone in the car, when there is no other noise, so I can truly "be still and know." I do hear from Him during my devotions, but they are far from the only time.

Psalm 139:7–10 says,

> Where can I go from your Spirit? Where can I flee from your presence? If I go up to the heavens, you are there; if I make my bed in the depths, you are there. If I raise on the wings of the dawn, if I settle on the far side of the sea, even there your hand will guide me, your right hand will hold me fast.

Deep, Soulful Places

Listening for His Voice

Listening is an art that is not mastered by many. It is the more difficult part of the communication process for most. It is one of the first things we teach families and couples when they come for counselling. It's hard to truly listen. We often hear, but we don't often listen, because we are too busy…too busy formulating our next thought, too busy planning our rebuttal, too busy with *us*. Listening involves focusing on the other person…noticing them, what words they are saying, *and* the meaning behind the words.

The art of listening to God is illustrated in the classic biblical story of Samuel and Eli, found in 1 Samuel 3. Eli was given charge of Samuel after Samuel's mom gave him to the temple—her part in her bargain with God: if He gave her a child, she would give him back to Him. Three times in the night, the Lord called to Samuel, and Samuel ran to Eli, thinking that Eli was calling him. After the third time, Eli realized that it must be the Lord who was calling Samuel and gave him direction as to how to answer when the Lord called again. And sure enough, the Lord did call again (because He never gives up on us). Samuel's answer: *"Speak, for your servant is listening."* The answer that warms the heart of God. It's the answer that I hope and pray I can say with more and more frequency as I do better at hearing Him when He speaks.

I'm embarrassed to say that I spent a good chunk of my younger years like Samuel—misattributing what God was saying to me and leading me to do to someone other than Him. I misattributed it to me—my professional training or the personal nature that He created me with. The number of times someone said "You always seem to call just at the right time" should have been a clue to me, but it wasn't. I just thought I had great timing. I didn't realize it was the Holy Spirit prompting me to call.

There are many reasons why I wasn't recognizing what was happening, the main one being that I wasn't practiced at it. I wasn't practiced at listening to God outside of Him speaking through His Word or through the preaching from the pulpit. I was brought up in a church where we focused on learning about and spending time with God in His Word and in prayer and believed that God would tell us things through His Word—and I feel that I did get good practice at that way of listening to Him. God's Word was (and is) definitely a lamp to my feet and light to my path (Psalm 119:105). But that was the only way of "hearing God" that I was practiced at.

I don't remember hearing about God speaking to us in other ways. Maybe I missed it. Regardless, I don't blame my church upbringing for me not recognizing

God's voice outside of His Word. But as a result, it took me some time, like Samuel, to wake up and know that in those other experiences it was God's voice, not my own, that I was hearing.

And that is the point. We need to practice hearing His voice and knowing that *He* is speaking...because He does, and will, speak to us. That is what happens when you are in a real relationship. It is not one-sided, with one person doing all the talking and the other person staying silent. It is a mutual experience where there is give and take, back and forth...reciprocity.

This is where some people start to get nervous. God speaking to us through His Word is not often argued. Using our closeness with Him as a way to help us understand Him better is also not often in dispute. But God actually speaking...like a real message directly to or for one person? That's not a thought always welcomed with open arms. But that is exactly what He wants me to highlight for you in this discussion; it's the reason for every single word I've been led to write up to this point.

In John 10:27, Jesus said that His sheep hear His voice. Isaiah 30:21 says, *"Whether you turn to the right or to the left, your ears will hear a voice behind you, saying, 'This is the way; walk in it.'"* John 15:26 says, *"When the Helper comes, whom I will send to you from the Father—the Spirit of Truth, who comes from the Father—he will testify on my behalf"* (ISV). Those verses are clear that we are able to *hear* Him and understand Him through the help of the Holy Spirit. How we "hear" Him may vary, as God is a personal God and He knows us well that He will speak in the way we will hear Him best.

There are countless examples of this through the Old and New Testaments, where God audibly spoke to His servants, to reveal Himself to them, to direct them and to help them in their relationship with Him, or He used a sign, spoke through someone or through some kind of vision. But always for the same ultimate purpose. And that purpose is the same today: intimacy with His children. God wants to talk with *you*. He wants to speak with *you*. He delights in that kind of intimacy with you. Because He loves you so much.

His Messages Are Unique and Personal

Some people get promptings from God that are very clear and that require bold action. Look at Noah. God asked something of him that certainly wasn't neat and tidy and socially acceptable. It was a big deal, it required much faith and effort from Noah, and he endured much ridicule in the process. But Noah had an intimate relationship with God, one where he knew Him because he spent lots of time with Him. As a result, when he heard God speak he knew for sure that it was Him, because he recognized Him. So he obeyed. I think it's important to highlight that because God speaks to each of us uniquely, we will all have our own way of hearing Him, so that when we are still, we *know* it's Him. I remember that when I used to ask people how you knew when you were in love, they would say, "When you know, you know." It would drive me nuts! Until I fell in love and realized that what they were talking about was true…when you know, you *do* know.

I have that same experience when it is God who is speaking to me. I get this sense of "knowing"—a deep resonance in my soul that I only get when it is Him speaking to me. As my relationship with Him grows, I do better and better at being tuned into that sense of knowing. I wish I could say that every time I know He speaks, I listen. But I don't. And I don't always slow down enough to hear, let alone listen. But thankfully that doesn't stop Him from talking.

I do think it's important that we are sure that it is *God* talking. That we are able to properly discern the difference between a good idea and a God-given idea. The difference between our desires and His. Psalm 37:4 says, *"Delight yourself in the LORD, and he will give you the desires of your heart"* (ESV). I don't think this means that if we do a good job of being close to God we will get what we want. Rather, what we want will be so in line with what He wants because of our time with Him and closeness to Him that His desires will become our desires. *We* start to want in our heart what *He* wants in our heart. And the more we spend time "doing life" with our God, the more He becomes a part of our every day, every moment, every breath, the more we will feel like we can hear Him and trust Him when we hear Him because of the relationship we have established with Him.

I also think it's important to recognize that we are human. So, even though we may have a deep sense of knowing that God is talking, like Jonah did, sometimes our heads can really get in the way of our souls. Heaven knows, I have that problem sometimes! We argue our way out of something—it's not rational, it's too risky, it couldn't really have been God, we must have heard wrong. Or, this is a big deal and I want, like Gideon with his fleece, to be sure—really sure—that it's Him.

Many people have come up with practical, tangible ways that you can use to help your head get in line with your soul on this topic, so I don't need to repeat them. And, quite frankly, what I would rather more than anything is for you to not be just in your head with this topic. Stay instead in the deep, soulful places that He is in, and listen to Him there…and trust Him.

He is God, beyond our full comprehension. But, as we look through the Bible, He spoke time and time again to people, and they *knew* it was Him. Not because they used certain tactics or tools designed to ensure they were hearing Him right, but because they listened and trusted in who was talking. Period. They paid attention to that deep resonance that occurs when we hear Him speak and didn't discount it. Noah, Moses, Gideon, the prophets…countless stories of times when God spoke and people listened. No manmade process designed to make sure. Just gut-level, soul-deep trust in Him that came from their knowledge and intimate experience of, and with, Him.

Are there people who don't hear Him right? Yes. Of course. Does the enemy tamper with our understanding of God so that we mess up the message? Yes. Do people project their preferences and desires onto God because they want what they want, not what He wants? Yes, unfortunately. But He can be heard by those who genuinely and purely want to hear *Him*. Because He is God. He doesn't need any help from us. He just needs us to say, "Speak; your servant is listening." And then actually listen.

It's about trusting in the truth of Proverbs 3:5–6: "*Trust in the LORD with all your heart, And lean not on your own understanding; In all your ways acknowledge Him, and He shall direct your paths*" (NKJV). Trust Him; don't rely on yourself. Acknowledge Him, and He will direct you. That's it. Three things we do, and He is faithful to respond. I think we get so caught up in theological debates and commentaries on the "right" way to communicate with Him that we lose the simplicity and truth that lies therein. Trust Him. He won't let you down.

Do you need to hear from Him? Talk to Him. Then listen, because He will answer. He may answer you by speaking directly to you. He may speak to someone else who has a message from Him for you, like the prophets from the Old Testament. He may speak to you through His Word. He may speak to you through an experience with Him. He may speak to you through a symbol. Or some other way. But He will speak. That is clear throughout Scripture. And it is for a very important reason. We are in a relationship with someone who *so* loves us.

I told you earlier about the retreat experience I had when I asked God to speak, told Him I was listening and then promptly fell asleep. When we got to the evening session that day, I started by asking if anyone had heard from God and wanted to share. One woman stood up and shared that she had gone for a walk in the woods and had come upon her dad's favourite flower, which happened to be quite rare. She had been really grieving the death of her parents that very morning, and so to have come upon that rare flower when she was listening for God to speak was to her a clear message from Him about His care for her in the midst of her grief. Another woman, who is an amazing artist, was also on a walk in the woods, and when she looked down, there at her feet was a single piece of wood, naturally formed in the shape of a cross. She was profoundly moved by this symbol, which felt to her to be a message of His love—a reminder in her artistic style that He did that—died on a cross—for her. He speaks to us. He knows what we need to hear from Him, and how. And He does it because He loves us.

Intimacy with Him Is Under Attack

The enemy of our souls would like nothing more than for us to not listen to God, because he is very threatened by believers who are tuned in to the voice of God. He works very, very hard to keep the noise in our lives so loud that we don't even realize we aren't listening or taking the time to listen. He's smart enough to do this in ways that are deeply impactful, while at the same time being incredibly subtle. He will do whatever it takes to distract us and undermine our understanding and experience of this.

He will try to attack our view of God, our understanding of His character and our view of ourselves in Christ. He can subtly pervert our belief that we have "heard God" into a belief that we are arrogant for thinking that we heard God. Or that we are crazy. Or a bit of both. He can get us focused on other explanations for God's voice that are completely plausible, so we never clue in to what is really going on. That is part of what was going on for me in my late teens and early twenties. I didn't make the link that those promptings to say and do things with my skills were *from God.*

Satan plagues us with counterarguments to the voice of God. Things like: it's not really Him; He wouldn't speak to you because of what you did or who you are; He knows you really aren't as good a Christian as you let people think you are…you are a phony, a fake; who are you to think that God could actually use you after all your failures, after all that you have done?; you are too damaged to be used by God; you haven't spent time with Him for days—you think He's going to speak to you?; you aren't like so and so—He speaks to people like her, not to people like you.

I could go on and on.

The thing about this kind of attack from Satan is that he knows the impact is personal and powerful. He is smart enough to know he can't stop God. Our lack of listening, whatever the reason, is not going to limit God or His plan in any given situation. But we can limit ourselves *in our own personal experience of Him* and

His desires for us. So that's what Satan works on. Remember the story of Jonah? Imagine the lies Satan was whispering into Jonah's ear: if you tell the people of Nineveh that message, you will be killed; run away, God won't keep you safe from them; He's sending you to do His dirty work and putting you in harm's way!

So Jonah runs. And it doesn't go well for him. No peace that passes all understanding guarding his heart and mind in Christ Jesus. No blessing and fulfillment from God being pleased with him. Just getting tossed overboard and swallowed by a big fish. Satan didn't include that part in his whisper of lies. He never does. *Because he doesn't care about us; he cares about ruining us.* In disobeying God, Jonah didn't stop God's purpose from being achieved. Not only did the people of Nineveh receive the message that God wanted them to hear, but Jonah delivered it. No, it wasn't God's plan that Jonah limited by not obeying. It was his experience of God's blessing and the intimacy with God that blessing brings. And as Jonah's story shows, in the end, obedience is what matters most. Like Jesus said in John 14:15, *"If you love me, keep my commands."*

There's a Purpose to Him Speaking

Every single time God spoke in the Bible, the purpose was ultimately connected to His relationship with His people. Every time. God doesn't just like to hear Himself talk. He doesn't just babble on like a chatterbox, leaving us to figure out why and what the point was. It always comes back to one fundamental fact...our relationship with Him matters to *Him.* That is why His messages to us are purposeful.

Sometimes He wants us to act as His "agent." There's something He is going to accomplish through us. There's a message He has for someone that we are to deliver, or there's something He wants us to do. Not that He couldn't do it Himself without us, because He could. But He always does what is best for us, and He knows there are times when using one of His servants for something will be far more impactful in ensuring that we realize just how important we are to Him and how real He wants to be in our world. I will give you a personal example to illustrate what I am talking about.

Like I told you earlier, when I'm drying my hair is a time when God speaks to me. A lot. Go figure! In this particular situation, a friend of mine had just had one of her close friends die in childbirth. The morning of the funeral as I was drying my hair, I distinctly felt God prompt me to call my friend and pray with her. I am embarrassed to admit that often when I would get these kinds of promptings while drying my hair, although I thought the ideas were good ideas, likely God moments, I would talk myself out of doing them: I have to get ready for work; the kids need food; I don't have time; it's too early to call, etc.

Remember Jonah? My head was getting in the way of my soul. This time the prompting was not ignorable, so I turned off the hair dryer and called my friend. When she answered, I said, "I was drying my hair and felt strongly led to call and pray for you, so that's why I'm calling," almost apologetically, as I knew she had a lot on her plate that day.

Her reaction is what has forever changed my responsiveness to the promptings I get while drying my hair. She burst into tears and said, "I was just sitting out here on my deck, with my Bible on my lap, feeling like I *should* pray, but not able to—not knowing what words to use. And then you called." That prompting from God was an opportunity for me to be God's agent to my friend. And it did not just reveal God's love to *her* in the midst of her pain; it blessed *me* and enriched my relationship with Him as I got to witness firsthand how personal and loving God is through His care for my friend in her grief. Because when you are loved, care is given. Needs are met. Wounds are attended to. He meets you there, where only He can go.

Lots of stuff can get in the way of our connection with God. In earthly relationships, busyness, distractions, stress, worry and complacency can drive a wedge in the intimacy we crave with others. The same can happen in our relationship with God. But because of His love for us, He is not content with that. He will initiate "conversations" with Him so that we can grow in our relationship with Him. It is up to us whether or not we respond, but He never stops trying to engage us. In my experience, and from what I can see in the Bible, He tends to do this primarily in one of two ways…either by pruning us (so that the things that get in the way of our intimacy with Him can be removed) or through a personal and intimate message to remind us of His love for us and how special we are to Him.

When He convicts us and prunes us, it is because of how much He loves us. He is not content to leave us as we are, because He knows that the more we are like Christ, the more wonderful our experience of Him will be and therefore the more wonderful our experience of life will be. I wish I could tell you that I'm unfamiliar with God's conviction in my life, but He regularly has to remind me of my sinfulness. Sometimes it is little stuff, and sometimes it is big.

When my oldest son, Ethan, was about 18 months old, he was an ongoing non-stop concern from when he awoke at six in the morning until bedtime. Naps, if they happened, lasted no more than 45 minutes at a time—but I could never be sure he'd sleep. So I couldn't do the typical "sleep when the baby sleeps" routine or follow the "get things done during his naps" advice I'd received. I had to get creative. As a result, during that time of his life my devotions often happened on our couch in the basement, with the stairs blocked off, while Ethan ran around like a ball of energy alternating between playing with toys, climbing on me and watching the odd snippet of a TV show.

One morning, I was doing a devotional on the story of Abraham and Isaac, where God tells Abraham to take his son up the mountain to offer him as a sacrifice. Talk about wanting to ensure you are hearing God correctly! I confess I've always had a hard time with that story. Before this day, I would often find myself wondering why God would put Abraham and Isaac through such a traumatic experience—the trauma of being asked to do such an act, the breech in the parent-child relationship and the attachment issues that Isaac would face afterward, to name just a few of the resulting implications.

As I sat reading the passage, half paying attention and half not, because it was one of those Sunday school stories I had heard so often that it was almost lost on me, I all of a sudden felt God clearly ask me "Would you do that for Me if I asked you to?" *What?!* Feeling very well trained in my Bible, I completely ignored answering the question at hand and instead responded with a detailed biblical rationale in my head for why that was not a valid question to begin with. Things like: that was the Old Testament; we live in resurrection times, where His sacrifice once for all was enough—that kind of sacrifice is not needed anymore; that was under the Old Covenant, but we are under the New Covenant. Therefore, God would never ask that of me.

But God wasn't satisfied with my head-knowledge response. He said, "I am not asking you for a theological discussion on *if* I would ask that of you now…I'm asking you, if I *did* ask you to do it for me now, would you do it?" I became very aware in that moment that my faith was being tested. My God was asking me to prove to Him that He alone held pre-eminence in my life. That no one and nothing else held His place in my heart. In asking me this, He was revealing to me that I had not fully given my son over to Him where he belonged—I was still holding on to that control.

I wish I could tell you that I immediately said, "Yes, of course I would, Lord," but that's not true. I didn't. Because I couldn't. I knew if I did, I was had. I was talking with God, who could see right to my heart, which was why He was asking me the question in the first place. So instead, I said, "I *want* to say yes, Lord, but I can't honestly do that in this moment—and You know my heart, so you know that it wouldn't be entirely true…but I *want* to. I want to say yes; I just can't."

And then I sat there being still with God for a while, tears streaming down my face, watching my precious little boy running around as God lovingly reminded me of who He is and how much I can trust Him. Specifically, He reminded me of the fact that He loves my child more than I ever could or would, and so if He asked something like this of me, I could trust His plan in that request. He reminded me that He will never leave me or forsake me. And then He gently told me that if I meant it that I loved Him more than anything, I had to be willing to show it—like He did for me.

By the end of my time on the couch that day, I was weeping and saying to Him, "Yes, Lord, I would do it if You asked me to, even though theologically I know You wouldn't. I trust You. You deserve my all, even my son." He was pruning and convicting me because He loved me *so* much, He didn't want anyone or anything getting in the way of our intimacy. Not because He wanted to cause me pain, but because He knows that when I am closest to Him, with nothing and no one in the way, my life is richest.

The other part of God speaking to us so that we can grow in our trust of and closeness with Him is when He does so to assure us of His love for us and His presence in our lives. So that we aren't left asking, "Is He really there? Does He really care?" These love messages from Him can be through something that is very personal and intimate, where we are confronted with the undeniable reality that it was Him speaking into our lives in a way that touches us deeply, or it can come through Him showing Himself in something practical—a clear directive like "This is what I want you to do." Or it can be both at the same time.

Regardless of how the message is conveyed, the result is that He provides us with a deepening in our experience of Him, of His day-to-day rubber-meets-the-road presence in our lives. And it draws us closer to Him, which is the whole point. Because when you love someone, you make sure that they know it…often, and without question.

I can't help but think of a friend of mine when I think of love messages from Him. And what is amazing is that His love messages to her have been both practical and tangible and also personal and intimate. My friend has been going through a serious unexplained illness—a season in life that would be considered "a valley" in spiritual terms, feeling like she is trudging along, trying to find higher ground. A life-threatening illness may send the faint at heart running for the hills, but not my friend.

Thankfully, my friend is a very godly woman. Her faith is deep, solid and secure. She knows God better than most, in my opinion. She has a really strong connection with Him and is very adept at talking to Him, listening to Him and hearing Him speak. Her relationship with God is such a testimony to me.

She has chosen to draw a line in the sand and to say that she trusts God, even amidst the deep pain that she is in. And she has chosen to trust that God will ultimately free her from this circumstance and restore her health, even though that seems like a really grand expectation right now.

My friend has chosen to believe this because she heard God tell her to expect this from Him. So she is. But you can imagine how hard that can be, when everything around her is pointing to the fact that she should scale back her expectations. A lot. But my friend knows God. She knows who talks to her. She knows His power. And she knows His voice. So she is trusting Him to be faithful.

Here's where His personal and intimate but practical and tangible love message comes in. I believe that God spoke to her because He wanted to make sure my friend had something to hold on to in the face of the lies of the enemy. He wanted to give her something to assure her of His undeniable love for her and His faithfulness to her, like an anniversary ring, a symbol that the promise that was made is still as real and special now as it was then.

One day, God laid on my heart that I was to tell her that God intended to heal her. It was a pretty grand expectation to tell her she was to have of Him. I actually typed it to her twice and erased it twice. It felt way too grand to say in the face of what she was mired in at the time (do you hear the lie of the enemy? I do). But God was very clear in His message, so I typed it a third time and also told her that had happened. The message was a message of hope. Of deliverance. Completely and fully. A pretty great expectation to place on God. But it was what He wanted said, so I said it. And, quite frankly, He can handle great expectations.

I confess that, because I'm still learning and growing in this area, I watched my phone constantly for her response. I felt so nervous about the message because of the magnitude of what I was putting on God by saying it. (Doesn't that sound ridiculous? Like somehow He can't handle the big stuff? What a lie.) Her response came very soon after I hit send. And it is forever etched on my soul.

She said thank you to me for listening to God and being obedient to Him. That He had been telling her the *exact* same message in her time with Him but that she had really needed to hear Him tell it to her from someone else, so that she could be sure that she was hearing from Him and not inferring her wishes and desires onto what she was hearing from Him. She *thought* she was hearing Him right, but given the seriousness of her illness and the magnitude of the message, she needed that extra sign that it was from Him. And He loves her *so* much that He knew that and gave her just what she needed…an immensely personal, intimate and specific message of love, a promise of hope from Him to her, and one that tangibly and practically addressed her situation on top of it all. What an amazing God.

Great Expectations

In Hebrews 4:16, the Bible says, *"Let us therefore come boldly to the throne of grace, that we may obtain mercy and find grace to help in time of need"* (NKJV). In another translation, it says to come before the throne of grace with confidence. He says we can be bold in what we come before Him with. He can handle it. That's actually the other really wonderful thing about a relationship with Him: having expectations isn't a bad thing; it is actually appropriate.

Not only can we be bold in our expectations of Him, but because of who it is that we are expecting things from, we can also rest assured that He won't let us down. I'm not saying that whatever we expect from Him we will get. But, Hebrews 10:23 says, *"Let us hold unswervingly to the hope we profess, for he who promised is faithful."* Our hope that we have is that He is faithful to be true to His character. He is who He says He is, and He will do what He promises to do, from the beginning to the end of time. Period. He never changes. So we can always expect Him to act in a way that reflects His character.

We can also expect His faithfulness to be demonstrated in a more personal, real way. That truth is at the crux of the statement to follow. Here it goes: I believe that God intends to speak to you. That He wants to speak to you. That He is actually longing to speak to you. And that if you want to hear from Him, He either already has spoken or will speak to you before you read the last word in this book. If you want to hear from Him. And if you are listening for His voice.

Jeremiah 29:13 says, *"You will seek me and find me when you seek me with all your heart."* That is His promise to us. That is His truth about Himself that He offers us. That is a great, bold expectation that you can have of Him to which He will be faithful to respond. And so I believe that before the end of this book, every single reader who seeks Him will find Him, who asks for Him will receive Him, who knocks on the door to have access to Him will have that door opened. I don't know how that will look for you, as God deals with each of His children uniquely. But I do know He is faithful, and if we ask Him to show up, He will. It is okay to have that kind of great expectation. It is befitting of Him.

I realize the possible implications that might come from that statement. That it might seem I am setting people up for disappointment. What if someone thinks that they haven't heard from Him? What if they finish the last page and hear silence? What if they are desperate for a word from God, and they close the book and feel like there wasn't even one letter, let alone one word, from Him? Believe me, I know all the things to be fretting about in making such a statement. But I have no choice. He told me to write it, so I need to.

I'm learning. When He speaks, listen. When He says to do something, do it. *Because when He says He will do something, He will do it.* It is not for me to alter His message, to cushion it, make it politically correct or more appealing or palpable to the hearer; it's just my job to convey the message. I confess to you, I don't always listen. Or I listen, but I think He needs my help—needs me to tweak His message or the timing a bit. Yikes. Good thing He is gracious and His mercies are new every morning (Lamentations 3:22-23, ESV)!

Here's a perfect example of what I mean: I was having lunch with a friend earlier this month. She had been in a prayer group where two of the leaders had said some things and behaved in such a way that she was left feeling uncared for and hurt by their actions. In her time with God she felt He had shown her what He wanted her to take from the experience, but she was unclear about why.

As I was driving home, I heard God tell me to instruct her to ask Him for clarity. So when I got home, I sent her a note. Only I felt a bit funny about telling her to ask Him for clarity, because I didn't want to offend her by implying through that statement that she hadn't already done so...so I decided I should alter God's message to her a bit. I know. How arrogant can I be? God's message needed my help. Ha! That is so embarrassing for me to admit to you. But it's the truth.

So the message I sent her was "God spoke to me about your situation. You need to ask Him *again* for clarity about why this keeps resurfacing." See the word *again?* My word, not His. Do you know what her response was? Her response was that despite all of the other questions she was led to ask Him about the situation, she had never actually asked for clarity about that particular point a first time. So I had to fess up and admit that wasn't actually His message for her. That *His* message was actually for her to ask Him for clarity. Period. Not *again.* That was my word.

Why do I share that with you? Two reasons. One is to illustrate just how intentional and specific He is with us. He knew what she needed and was happy to have her ask Him for it. So much so that when it seemed she wasn't going to ask spontaneously on her own, He nudged her to do so. Because His love for her (and all His children) meant He didn't want her unclear when He had the answer she needed. The other reason is to offer you a real-life personal (albeit embarrassing) example of why it is so important to listen to Him when He speaks and to do exactly what He is asking of you. He knows what He is doing…way more than you or I do! Because He can handle the great expectations He encourages us to place on Him, when we hear Him tell us to be bold we need to be bold and then wait and watch Him move.

Now, it really isn't bold to suggest that God will speak to you if you want to hear Him. It is just a fact about our God. *He* says He will speak to us if we are listening. That's not a new idea on my part. I'm not stating anything about God that He hasn't already stated about Himself, both in terms of His actual descriptions about Himself and in His behaviours and actions towards those He loves. So it's not really bold at all. It just *is*.

But I suspect I am not the only one who might think it bold to make such a statement. And I suspect that the enemy of our souls would rather we not have those kinds of expectations of God, because he knows how powerful they are. He would rather us scale it back and think that we can't really expect God to do what He says He will do, especially if it is big. What a lie. This too is one of those deep, soulful places He reaches into when we open our eyes and ourselves up to Him.

Because, at the root of it all, this is an intimate relationship He offers you. One where He speaks to you. One where the seemingly small, insignificant details matter to Him. One where spending time with Him allows you to know Him more. One where His messages are real and unique to you. One where He cares enough to swoop into the everyday and show Himself. Because He is faithful. Because you matter to Him, and He is desperate to speak to you. He longs for you to hear from Him. Because He *so* loves you.

CHAPTER SEVEN

Love Means No Fear

There is no fear in love. But perfect love drives out fear,
because fear has to do with punishment. The one who
fears is not made perfect in love.

1 John 4:18

I'm alone, and it's dark. I'm almost at my car, which is uncharacteristically parked in a secluded and dimly lit spot. As I near my car, I notice a suspicious man lurking. I quicken my pace, feigning ignorance to his presence and the rapidly decreasing gap between us. His eyes lock with my gaze, and I am forced to accept that I am in real danger and need to act fast. I try to run to my car door as he leaps towards me, but I can't make my body move. My mouth is open, and I am trying to scream with all my might, but no sound will come from my mouth. I wake up, covered in sweat, tears streaming down my face. Why do I keep having this dream? It hasn't happened to me in real life, but it sure feels like it has, long after I waken. What is it that causes me to dream this night after night, like a scene from the movie *Groundhog Day*?

I'm afraid. Fear is something I've fought against all my life. I fear losing someone I love, again. And so I fear losing control. I fear being exposed. I fear I will be taken advantage of in my areas of vulnerability. Before I figured out how my early life experiences had shaped me and nurtured and fostered my fears, I used to also fear making someone angry or disappointing them. I feared rejection and failure. If I let it, the fear of losing someone I love could still rule me today like it used to.

Some would argue that fear is a good thing—if we didn't have a healthy fear of danger, for example, we would be at risk of getting hurt. Fight or flight. They would say that fear keeps you safe. Others would say that we are to fear God and would quote quite a few verses to support this claim, like Psalm 111:10, *"The fear of the LORD is the beginning of wisdom."* I don't disagree.

But that's not the kind of fear I'm talking about, and it's not the kind that perfect love drives out (1 John 4:18). Because that is the good side of fear. It's more of a healthy reverence or respect for someone or something.

The kind of fear that God's love drives out and frees us from is the kind that had me trapped. The kind that could easily trap me again if I let it. It's the kind of fear that immobilizes, controls and undoes you. It robs you of joy. Of peace. Of confidence and a desire to grow and learn. It does not resemble a healthy reverence or respect at all. It's an unhealthy leech that sucks the life right out of you. It's a weapon in the arsenal of he who seeks to kill and destroy.

The fact that God's love casts out fear is a powerful reality. It meets me in a very deep place and resonates in my soul. There is a place where I do not have to be afraid. Where there is nothing bad that can rob me of the good. Where I don't have to be on my guard. Where I am able to be vulnerable, exposed and raw and know with certainty that I do not need to fear the consequences of that kind of intimacy. Ultimately, God made us that way, in need of a safe place. And it is a need to be filled by Him, and Him alone.

There are lots of things to fear in this world these days. And things seem to be getting worse in our society—shootings in schools, bullying that leads to suicides, terrorist attacks that cause mass death and destruction. Life requires constant mental gymnastics to ensure we don't get sucked into the vortex of worry that comes from the reality of the world we live in. Anxiety disorders are a dime a dozen. In fact, we began to see so many referrals for children struggling with anxiety at my place of work, we developed a group for children with anxiety to help them cope, because we couldn't keep up with the demand of seeing each child individually. I don't think it is a coincidence that we are seeing an increase in anxiety in people at the same time as what is happening in the world around us.

Some fears have been around since the beginning of time. Fear of abandonment, fear of rejection, fear of failure and even fear of a person. Unfortunately, because of other human beings there is also fear of God. We attribute to God qualities that have been demonstrated by others, and the result can be great fear of Him.

I don't think God ever intended for things to be like this. When He created the earth back at the beginning of time and pronounced it good, it was good. There was nothing to be afraid of. Nothing to worry about. Nothing to have to be cautious about or guard against. But then sin entered the world, and it has been all downhill since then. With each passing year our world drifts farther away from His original, perfect creation. However, because He loves us *so* much, He has created a safe place for us in relationship with Him. A place where all the things that chip away at our foundation of trust, hope and safety don't apply. Where all the relationship problems we see around us don't occur. Where we are safe, secure and unconditionally loved. Where there is nothing to fear.

Please don't misunderstand me. I'm not saying that if you are loved by God and you feel fear, there is something wrong with you. Nor am I saying that if you are in a relationship with God you will never be afraid. Like I mentioned before, there are many things in this world to legitimately be afraid of. Bad things happen, without reason, warning or rationale, all the time. We live in a fallen world, and are surrounded by evidence of that on a daily basis. And there is that "good side" to fear that alerts us to danger.

What I *am* saying is that God, and what He offers us in relationship with Him, is safe. That although there may be valid reasons to be afraid of people or things or experiences in the world around us, what we have with *Him* is not one of them. *He* will never leave us. Never hurt us. Never abandon us. Never condemn us. Never let us down. Never turn His back on us. Never lead us astray. Never reject us. Never treat us unfairly. Never victimize us. Never do anything to us that we have to worry about in our day-to-day lives *outside* of our relationship with Him.

And, because He never lets us down, we can go to Him when the world is swirling around us and we are feeling threatened to be overtaken by fear. He promises us, in Him, that we don't have to be afraid. In fact, the Bible is full of times when God said, "Do not be afraid." It wasn't always because the perceived threat was not real. He often said it when someone was facing attack, torment or certain death. The danger was real. But He said it because He promised to be there with them. So they wouldn't be alone. So they would not be in the deep, the hard, the confusing and the painful by themselves.

I love Isaiah 35:4 because the words are so powerful and strong, and they speak right into that place in me that would so easily be all-consumed by fear. It says, *"Say to those with fearful hearts, 'Be strong, do not fear; your God will come, he will come with vengeance; with divine retribution he will come to save you.'"*

This is where the rubber meets the road. It touches the most tender, vulnerable parts of us. Few people have had nothing cause them serious pain. Many have had more than their fair share. Many who would say to Isaiah, "No, He won't come. He didn't in my life." Maybe you feel that way. You cried out to Him. You asked for His help, and the bad stuff continued all the same. You sought Him, and you feel like you didn't find Him; you found hurt. You were desperate to be rescued, and yet the situation remained the same.

How can God tell us to not be afraid and then do nothing to change the hard situation? How can God promise to come with vengeance and bring divine retribution, and yet it seems like the evil and corrupt are getting ahead and those who are doing things the right way are struggling? Those are very good questions, to which there are no simple answers. My prayer is that God would meet you where you are and that you would encounter Him and see how He is coming with a vengeance in your life, how He is working out His divine retribution in your situation. He is actually there for you in the midst of whatever this life is throwing at you. You can experience someone loving you *so* much that He stands with you in the deepest of deep, the hardest of hard and the most fear-provoking situations you could imagine.

He Always Shows Up

Faithfulness is at the core of what God offers us in relationship with Him. He ensures that He will never leave us or forsake us. It makes it safe to be vulnerable with Him because nothing in Him *should* cause us to fear. And yet, this is not what many people feel. They are not sure whether God will "show up" in a given situation. And this is one of Satan's most common and powerful ploys to undermine our trust and confidence in God's faithfulness.

The Bible is very clear about God's faithfulness to us. Some of the verses we talked about in the previous chapter spoke very specifically of that. But this particular topic deserves a bit more concentrated attention, in light of how often it is attacked by the enemy. So, let's focus on just a few verses from the New Testament—mostly ones that came right from Jesus Himself during His time on earth. Verses on God's promise to show up.

In Matthew 7:7 Jesus says, *"Ask and it will be given to you; seek and you will find; knock and the door will be opened to you."* John 14:13 says, *"And I will do whatever you ask in my name, so that the Father may be glorified in the Son."* And then in 1 John 5:14–15, John writes, *"This is the confidence we have in approaching God: that if we ask anything according to his will, he hears us. And if we know that he hears us—whatever we ask—we know that we have what we asked of him."* Pretty specific, clear verses that state we can have confidence that He hears us and responds. That when we seek Him we will find Him. That He will show up when we ask or need Him to.

Those of you who feel you have not experienced this truth in your lives may be ready to stop this discussion right here. I get that. There is woundedness and pain that often accompanies us seeking after God. He meets us in those deep, soulful places. He goes right there, right in the midst of the pain, hurt and wound-edness, and offers us something we need there. Himself. He has something for you in those places, just as He has something for me.

Back to the verses. Sometimes people feel those verses are describing a vending-machine God: put in a dollar, make your selection and get a bag of chips. Put in a request, get what you asked for from God. And while God shows all through His Word that He has the *ability* to provide specific answers to specific requests, in light of His character, that is not what those verses are saying. Those verses speak to our experience of Him in relationship. They speak to our closeness to Him, to our desire to know Him and have Him show up in our lives.

In my experience, and in my words, this is what these verses mean: "Ask for my personal presence in your life and you will receive it; seek Me and you will find Me; Knock on the door to My presence and I will open it for you and let you come in and be closer to Me" (see Matthew 7:7). "And I will do whatever you ask in my name—whatever will enhance our relationship with each other and my reputation with those around you, so that God can be glorified" (see John 14:13). "This is the confidence we have in approaching God: that if we ask anything according to His will, according to what will bring us closer to Him and His desires for our life, He hears us. And if we know that He hears us, if we are in relationship with Him such that we are truly listening to Him—whatever we ask that is an outgrowth of our love for Him and that desire to get closer in relationship to Him—we know we have what we have asked of Him" (see 1 John 5:14–15).

Jeremiah 29:13 promises, *"You will seek me and find me when you seek me with all your heart."* Have you done that? There is tremendous power, strength, help and hope for everyone who applies those verses. Because they mean taking our eyes off our circumstances and the chaos swirling around us and putting them on Him. And just as I experienced amidst my worst life experiences, you too can know He's keeping His promises and showing up.

I know this because my family has lived it.

When I was three and a half, my parents and I were having a sleepover at my dad's parents' house in Scarborough. My grandparents lived in a multi-split-level home. You walked in the front door, and the foyer was floor one. You went up five steps to the "main floor," which had the kitchen and living and dining rooms. To your right, you could go up about seven steps to a bathroom and two bedrooms or down about seven steps to a bathroom and two more bedrooms, and then down again seven steps to the finished basement. This was like a castle to a three and a half year old; and with so many places for the boogey man to hide, it was scary to me. It was especially scary because my parents and I slept on different floors. My parents slept upstairs in what I called "the pink room," which was aptly named for its pink carpet, pink curtains, pink wallpaper and pink bedspread. The other bedroom upstairs was my grandma's. She snored like a trucker, so no one slept with her. Not even my grandpa. He slept downstairs, across from "the purple room"—and you can imagine why I used to call it that, only add to your visual a hanging light over the bed that was a cluster of purple grapes! Interestingly, my grandpa snored like a trucker too.

On this particular night, I woke up in the middle of the night with bad dreams. I look back now and think how could I not have bad dreams, with a giant pile of grapes hanging over my head! My mom came down and slept with me, to comfort me and so I wouldn't wake everyone else up.

In the morning, my dad didn't come down. Eventually, my mom went to wake him, but he wouldn't wake up. She describes, in those first moments of going into the room and not being able to wake him, not wanting to believe it but knowing he was dead.

My mom was raised in the Gospel Hall, an ultra-conservative Brethren assembly. She wasn't allowed to cut her hair, wear pants, have a TV or listen to radio except for certain Christian channels. It was a very strict, conservative and cerebral denomination. There was no emotionalism. So, when she saw my dad was dead and she felt a tingling sensation from the top of her head to the tips of her toes, she says it was unlike anything she'd ever experienced. She says she instantly knew it was the Holy Spirit infusing her with His power to cope with the minutes, hours, weeks and years to come. She never experienced something like that again, but she recognized it as the Holy Spirit, as clear as the nose on her face.

She describes knowing that she would survive as she sat beside my dad, with reality undeniable before her, because God had made His presence, His strength and power known to her in that moment. *He had helped her feel Him in every cell of her body.* And in the dark, desperate days that followed as my brother was born a week later—one and a half months premature—she did it. It wasn't easy, and she was *deeply* grieving, but she could do it.

How? Because of God. Because He says in Hebrews 13:5, *"Never will I leave you; never will I forsake you."* Never. He always shows up, and He never leaves.

If you asked my mom, she would tell you that my dad was the love of her life. He was all she could have ever dreamed of. And when he died at 29, he left a wake of people searching for the *why.* She would also tell you that God is bigger than that, that He is faithful…and that she is living proof of that truth.

God didn't bring my dad back to life, although I know that was my mom's heart's desire. But He showed up. Because when you are in relationship with Him and you don't even know how to ask for Him or aren't even aware of how much you need Him yet but you still listen for Him in whatever way He chooses to reveal Himself, He *will* be found. He will open that door and let you in. He may choose a way like He did with my mom. He may do it through a friend, like He did prompting me to call my friend when I was drying my hair. He may do it in a service at church. Or through something you read. But He always shows up.

It was not His will that my dad continue to live—I don't get why, and I won't until heaven. But it was His will that my mom survived. That she knew Him. That she received His presence. That she had an open door to Him. That she found Him time and time again, and that she was always able to remember that feeling of Him and His presence that horrible day. God never promised my mom that she would be married to my dad for decades, although certainly that is what they expected when they said their vows. He didn't promise her that she wouldn't have hardships in her life. He promised He'd be there. He would never leave her. And He fulfilled those promises. Not only that, He made sure she never wondered whether or not He left her in her darkest moment. Before she even had the *chance* to seek Him, cry out and find Him, He had already wrapped His arms around her to carry her through.

Believe it or not, my mom had well-meaning but *very* misguided Christians ask her what horrible sins my dad did to be taken away from this earth at such a young age. If that were a true reflection of God and the way He deals with His children, we all would have been in heaven by age two! People want to feel immune from "senseless" tragedy. But that is not how God or the world works. We are living in a fallen world, so bad stuff is going to happen. And God is God and doesn't always make sense to us. He doesn't promise otherwise. He just promises to show up, *despite* the bad stuff and *in the midst* of the bad stuff.

Yes, God performs miracles and provides tangible answers to specific requests. He is the same God of the Bible, and I don't discount that at all. I pray for miraculous answers all the time. All I am saying is that immunity from death and suffering is not what "*I will never leave you nor forsake you*" means (Hebrews 13:5, NKJV). If it was, there would be a lot of people that God was lying to.

Circumstances do not always give us a good understanding of God's faithfulness or how He is fulfilling His promises to His children. Circumstances are a lot like feelings: they are real, but they aren't always right, and they can lead us astray. When we look solely at the tangible to find Him, we may miss Him.

And when we measure His love for us based on how good things are for us, we could be led very far astray.

Satan Doesn't Like God's Faithfulness

Since misrepresenting God and His faithfulness is one of the ways the enemy robs us of intimacy with Christ, he wants us to see our situations as "proof" of God not showing up. But my mom's story demonstrates that He *always* shows up, even when we don't cry out to Him. Even in the most tragic of situations. He didn't bring my dad back to life. He didn't reverse the hands of time and change that deadly night. And that was in the face of many people praying as my dad was rushed to the hospital. Many deeply faithful God-loving believers all over the Greater Toronto Area prayed fervently that God would save him. But He didn't. Yet my mom knows with certainty that God showed up. That, in fact, He never left.

Satan wants to take God's perceived silence or inactivity and twist it to trigger our fears. *He is not faithful. He abandoned you. It's because you don't measure up. God doesn't love you as much as others. He isn't as present as everyone wants to think...* The lies are varied and endless.

The enemy also wants us to believe that we have to be careful about what we say God is capable of. He knows how faithful God is and the power that is unleashed when we choose to believe that God will show up. So he works hard to undermine our confidence in claiming this promise for people. Especially people in pain. Have you ever heard this lie whispered in your ear? "Don't say that, what if it doesn't happen? What will that do to their faith?" I have.

How could we possibly be setting anyone up for disappointment by saying that God will show up and will be faithful in being found when sought?

> What, then, shall we say in response to these things? If God is for us, who can be against us? He who did not spare his own Son, but gave him up for us all—how will he not also, along with him, graciously give us all things?...Who shall separate us from the love of Christ?...For I am convinced that neither death nor life, neither angels nor demons, neither the present nor the future, nor any powers, neither height nor depth, nor anything else in all creation, will be able to separate us from the love of God that is in Christ Jesus our Lord. (Romans 8:31–32, 35, 38–39)

Nothing can separate us from His love. Your circumstances are not proof that you are not loved. Don't listen to those lies. We may have to live in this fallen world right now, but He won't leave us. He stays here with us. He helps us. He gives us strength as we seek it from Him, and He shows up. To attempt to "explain" why the bad things happen cheapens the reality of challenging experiences. Why do bad things happen and why doesn't He answer the way we hope? It's hard to understand why He answers some people some ways and other people in different ways.

Sometimes it can help to find someone you trust who can seek Him with you. When two or more people are gathered seeking Him on something specifically, He has promised to be there (Matthew 18:20). And without knowing your situation, I can tell you this: He doesn't want you to fear. He wants to be found by you. He will answer you, and although you may be looking for Him to answer in a different way than He does, that doesn't mean He isn't answering. His ways aren't our ways, and His thoughts are not like our thoughts (Isaiah 55:8). It doesn't mean He isn't helping, strengthening and working all things together for good for those who love Him (Romans 8:28). Sometimes we have to change how we are looking for Him—what we are using as evidence of Him.

Daniel Shows Us How

Look at Daniel. He was obeying God. He was following God's rules, not the rules of the misguided king. If anyone should have been given favour by God, Daniel should have. But when Daniel stood firm in his faith and convictions about what was right, what happened? He was thrown in a den of lions, to be eaten alive. Talk about a fear-provoking situation!

Have you felt you were in a lion's den, facing the prospect of being eaten alive? Maybe you have stared into the drooling jaws of a flesh-eating monster ready to completely devour you. I've talked with many people who have. And I know the experience was terrifying. Worthy of fear, if you ask me. Can't say I'd be puffing out my chest all strong and confident in the face of that kind of scenario. But what if God wants us to? What if He wants us to puff out our chests, strong and confident *in Him?* Despite our circumstances. Because He is the God of the universe, and He can do anything.

Remember what happened to Daniel when he did that? Absolutely nothing. He was completely unharmed. He testified the next day to the king who threw him in there that God sent His angel and shut the lions' mouths. (The whole story is in Daniel 6.) Daniel had every reason to presume that God's promises wouldn't apply to him. Because he was being subjected to manipulation by some powerful jealous advisors and sentenced to death, it would have been easy to see his circumstances as hopeless and believe the lies of the enemy. But he didn't. He trusted in the truth, in who he knew God to be. He chose to look for God in whatever way He chose to show Himself. He didn't focus only on being in a den of lions. He determined that his circumstance was not reason to feel abandoned.

No matter how circumstances unfold or how it seems God isn't showing up, wait. Trust. He is…maybe just in a different way, in a different timing than perhaps you desire.

After the lion experience, Daniel experienced more with God—like visions and prophecies about the brutal fate of the kings he served—that required faith that he heard God correctly and could count on Him to do as He said He would do. What do you think Daniel's confidence-in-God-and-His-faithfulness meter reading was after the lions' den episode? I'd guess 10 out of 10. So when God said, *"Do not be afraid"* (Daniel 10:19), Daniel knew with certainty that it was safe to trust Him and could say in response, *"Speak, my Lord, since you have given me strength"* (Daniel 10:19).

Daniel had profound experiences with God, often in the face of bleakness and seemingly certain death. God doesn't waste anything. He can take what seems all evil and use it for our good. Such is His power.

Daniel is like Joseph, whose brothers sold him into slavery out of jealousy (which is kind of on the evil side, if you ask me!), and yet he ended up becoming a ruler who saved his entire family *and* the nation from famine because God redeemed the situation. Joseph said to his brothers, who were rightly trembling in fear, *"You intended to harm me, but God intended it for good to accomplish what is now being done, the saving of many lives"* (Genesis 50:20).

Have you noticed in your life how making it through a significant struggle teaches you about God's strength and comfort so that you can rely on it and experience it further in other situations? Out of the rotten, He's made something good? Look for it in your life, and you will find it.

That is ultimately what He promises. Not that life will be perfect. Not that He will prevent the ills of the world from happening, but that He will be with us and strengthen us. He will not abandon us. He will give us what we need to survive. Are you surviving? Are you making it? Maybe just by the skin of your teeth? Yet can you find Him there with you, holding on to you? Do you see how He has not left you? He loves us *so* much that we don't have to fear being left.

It might feel like it. I get that. But that is not His desire for you. He doesn't want you to fear Him, and He doesn't want you to fear what's going on in your life.

The enemy does, and he wants us paralyzed. Discouraged. Disillusioned. Then we aren't a threat. God knows that if we're too afraid we won't follow where He's asking us to go, regardless of the destination. So He goes before us. He surrounds us and sustains us. He gives us all we need to live in joy and fullness and escape pain and despair.

At a time when I was feeling alone in my struggle, God used the following set of verses to speak to me powerfully about His presence there with me. I knew in my heart it was Him. I share them with you in the hopes that they may be of encouragement to you as well:

> God is my defense. The LORD is my rock and my fortress and my deliverer; the God of my strength, in whom I will trust; my shield and the horn of my salvation, my stronghold and my refuge; my Savior. The LORD is my strength and my shield; my heart trusted in Him, and I am helped; therefore my heart greatly rejoices, and with my song I will praise Him. When the enemy comes in like a flood, the Spirit of the LORD will lift up a standard against him. We may boldly say: 'The Lord is my helper; I will not fear. What can man do to me?' The LORD is my light and my salvation; whom shall I fear? The LORD is the strength of my life; of whom shall I be afraid? As the mountains surround Jerusalem, so the LORD surrounds His people from this time forth and forever. Because You have been my help, therefore in the shadow of Your wings I will rejoice. For Your name's sake, lead me and guide me." (Psalm 59:9, 2 Samuel 22:2–3, Psalm 28:7, Isaiah 59:19, Hebrews 13:6, Psalms 27:1, 125:2, 63:7, 31:3, NKJV)[3]

I was struggling, and I felt alone. Then I opened up my devotions, and God pointed me to these verses. He showed up for me in a way that He knew would matter to me. God might use something different for you—a call from a cherished friend, a timely card in the mail, the perfect song at the perfect moment— but God always speaks.

---

[3] Anne Graham Lotz, *Daily Light* (Nashville: J. Countryman, 1998).

Deep, Soulful Places

What about Abuse?

We can't talk about fear without mentioning abuse. Any kind of abuse causes fear in the person being abused. The Bible is often used to justify abuse in the name of godliness, but love protects; it doesn't abuse (1 Corinthians 13). Anyone who claims their abusive treatment of others is justified is distorting the truth and spewing lies. First John 4:7 says, *"Dear friends, let us love one another, for love comes from God."* Love comes from God and is sanctioned by God. Not pain, abuse or torment. Love is patient; love is kind. It does not hurt or cause anyone to feel "less than." No one has any authority to be abusive in God's eyes. Ever. Yet many people live in fear…fear for their own lives, fear of retribution, even fear of God because of how people in authority have treated them. While it is understandable to feel this way, it is important to emphasize that this treatment is not reflective of the heart of a loving God for you.

If you have experienced abuse as a child or are experiencing it as an adult, I have devoted appendix F to some additional thoughts on this topic. But before we finish with the subject of fear, let me just say this: Don't allow yourself to be deceived by the enemy into putting onto God the "love" you experienced in your intimate relationships or your childhood. He doesn't want you to be hurt. He doesn't want you to think that abuse of any kind is okay. You are not hopeless; you are not stuck with a loveless life. He wants you to feel His love. He wants to meet you in those deep wounded places and offer you hope and healing. No strings attached. Out of His character. Out of His love for you. Because that is who He is. He is love.

And because He is love, He wants you to know that He will never leave you. That you are worth enough to Him for Him to stay with you in the deep, soulful places. That, like He said in Isaiah 35:4, *"Be strong, do not fear; your God will come, he will come with vengeance; with divine retribution he will come to save you."*

He *will* come. He always shows up. He never leaves. And it is for that reason that we do not need to fear. Because there is no fear in love, and perfect love casts out fear (1 John 4:18). And you are *so* loved, by the one and only true, perfect, Almighty God. So loved.

CHAPTER EIGHT

Love Means We Are Cherished

"For you are a holy people, who belong to the Lord your God. Of all the people on earth, the Lord your God has chosen you to be his own special treasure."

Deuteronomy 7:6 (NLT)

Around the time I started writing, my eight-year-old, Caleb, asked what my book was about. I tried to explain this topic (which has taken me nine chapters to discuss in book format!) in eight-year-old language in a few sentences, and I mentioned something about being cherished by God. This led to him asking me what *cherished* meant. I did my best to explain it to him—I suggested that when you cherish something, it means it's a treasure to you; it's something that means so much to you that you don't want to let it go; it holds such value that it is very, very special to you.

"Does that make sense, buddy?" I asked.

"I think so," he answered. "You mean it's like how I feel about you."

Talk about melting my heart! That kid is going to have the women wrapped around his little finger with his sweet-talking, that's for sure. To have my son feel that way about me is enough to keep me going for a while. To have anyone express that kind of emotion towards you is a pretty amazing feeling…melt-worthy!

That's how God feels about us. Actually, that's the tip of the iceberg of how God feels about us! His is not the kind of "love you" that gets thrown around as nonchalantly as "How are you?" No, it's the kind of love that caused Him to send His Son to die for us. The kind of love that makes Him continue to pursue us, every last part of us, because He is not content with "merely" saving us. It's the kind of love that studies us. Knows us. Wants to be with us. Works all things together for good for us. Promises to always be there for us. Considers us a treasure that means so much, He doesn't want to let go, because we hold such value.

That kind of cherished.

Deep, Soulful Places

Deuteronomy 7:6 speaks so beautifully of this truth. *"For you are a holy people, who belong to the Lord your God. Of all the people on earth, the Lord your God has chosen you to be his own special treasure"* (NLT). I love the words *"God has chosen you to be his own special treasure."* Imagine…the God of the universe choosing you as His treasure. Choosing me. As His *treasure.* That is such a moving, touching description to me. It goes beyond the standard Church language about God loving and saving us from sin to the deep places we long to have met. He chose us…as His treasure.

I realize that this may feel like a logical connection—being loved makes you feel cherished. If so, you have had at least one earthly relationship where love made you feel truly special and valued. But you may not have had that kind of love. So many people have never seen selfless love, and that has made it nearly impossible to feel even remotely cherished.

Even many who *have* been blessed by this kind of love have not stopped to think about the fact that it applies to our relationship with God. Or they've thought about it and conceptualized it in their heads, but it is difficult to grasp in their hearts. Many Christians who have had longstanding personal relationships with Christ struggle to conceptualize in a feeling, soul-level way what this love means—to be cherished by God. It's hard to really absorb into the fibres of our beings that He literally sacrificed His Son for us. That doesn't happen in our society today, so although in our heads we can "do the math" of what that means (sacrifice of only Son = big demonstration of love), it's an intellectual concept rather than an experiential reality. We have no real time frame of reference, so it stays as a concept in our heads; and because of that, the real life present-day relational, emotional and soul-level application that He cherishes us is lost.

While I understand that this verse in Deuteronomy is talking about the Israelites, who have been marked as God's chosen ones, I also think it applies to you and me. New Testament passages that reference Christians in general echo the sentiments of Deuteronomy. In 1 Peter 2:9 we read, *"But you are a chosen people, a royal priesthood, a holy nation, God's special possession, that you may declare the praises of him who called you out of darkness into his wonderful light."* There is that language again…*chosen, special, His.* God's special possession. A treasure. That is true love, if you ask me. Love that goes beyond our imagination.

It's helpful to remember that because God never changes, what He said to His people at the beginning of time still stands today. Because of Jesus, we are also His chosen people through the New Covenant. So when He is speaking these beautiful words through His prophets in the Old Testament, we can appreciate that this message is for us as well.

We are still God's. And He is still God. The character traits of God in the Old Testament, requiring the laws to be followed, are the same traits of God of the New Testament, who sent His Son to die. It all ties together in Him, in His love. His messages then and now and His character then and now all come together as important parts of the love letter He has left us in His Word. And what we are clearly told is that it means we are His treasure. His special possession. We are cherished.

I have a friend who was recently doing some work with God on some of the past and present hurts in her life. This friend has been such a testimony to me about the power of faith in the face of trials. Her faith is beautiful, and her ability to see His hand in the midst of the pain is something I can only hope to emulate. During the healing process, He gave her a very clear picture of His love and intentions for her. The picture was of a decadent table prepared for her in a beautiful valley. A symbol that despite the mountains she has had to climb, He *does* have good things for her.

The other day I was reading Psalm 23 and was completely taken by verse 5, which says, *"You prepare a table before me in the presence of my enemies."* Never before had I stopped to consider what it meant to have Him prepare a table for me in front of my enemies, but as I felt led to write and share this verse with my friend, the significance of that act was impressed on my heart.

Picture it with me. There is God, preparing a table full of good things for my friend. She is so cherished by Him that not only is He drawing her close, He wants to spend time with her at a special table *He* has prepared just for her. Her enemies, and *the* enemy, are all around, watching with envy and jealousy as each piece of cutlery made of pure silver and each piece of fine china is carefully laid in her honour. As each succulent gourmet dish is placed with love on the table, her enemies can't take it anymore. They want to rob her of this too.

But God stops them. And as He sends them away, He says, "No. This is just for My cherished daughter. I love her, and this is what I have prepared for *her.* Not you. You are not allowed to touch or taint this table of love and good things that I have for her." Then He turns to my friend, in the presence of her enemies, and says, "You may share with them if you'd like, but only after I have filled you and you have received from Me the good I have for you."

Imagine the vindication and the righting of so many wrongs that occurs at that table prepared just for her, in front of all her enemies. The healing and nourishment there for her. The blessing, richness and love. Because of how He cherishes her. How He cherishes you and me.

God Is Jealous (Zealous) for You

One of God's traits is His jealousy for us. And that is a good thing. A very good thing. You may be wondering how there could be a good kind of jealous. If you asked me as a therapist, I would tell you it's a red flag, indicative of insecurity. It suggests a lack of trust and a lack of self-esteem. I would tell you that in a healthy relationship, there is no place for jealousy and no need for it. Period.

So, how is a jealous God considered a good thing?

In fact, not only is He described as a jealous God in Exodus 34:14, it is one of His names! That is not a name you find in many praise songs! But it's clearly stated: *"Do not worship any other god, for the Lord, whose name is Jealous, is a jealous God."*

Merriam-Webster Online defines *jealous* as:

- 1a: intolerant of rivalry or unfaithfulness
- b: disposed to suspect rivalry or unfaithfulness
- 2: hostile toward a rival or one believed to enjoy an advantage
- 3: vigilant in guarding a possession

It gives *possessive* as a synonym. It also suggests that it is a more modern version of the old English word *zealous,* which means "marked by fervent partisanship for a person, a cause, or an ideal: filled with or characterized by zeal [ardent interest in pursuit of something: fervor]."

How could a perfect, all-powerful, ever-present, all-knowing God be jealous? There's no one like Him! You would think someone like that would have healthy self-esteem and confidence. The thing is, God's jealousy is about his zeal for, fervour for and ardent interest in us. He knows exactly who He is, and He knows who the "other man" is and how powerfully that enemy can persuade us to keep a part of ourselves from Him and suffer as a result.

God's jealousy for us is because He cherishes us. Because He is possessive of us. We *are* His treasure that if He ever let go of would be lost. We are very, very special to Him. And, He is vigilant in guarding us, because He knows that there is a hostile enemy out there trying to take advantage of us, trying to lure us away, trying to rival Him for our attention.

God's jealousy is selfless; He is filled with zeal for us. He pursues us. He wants us for Himself. And this is a good thing. This is the best thing for us. God's jealousy does not smother and control us, like jealousy in human relationships. His jealousy sets us free. Because the more we are ardently pursued and vigilantly possessed by the God of the universe in combat against the rivalry of the kingdom of darkness, the less chance there is that we will get caught in a snare.

God is supposed to be first in our lives. And that actually keeps everything else in balance, rather than throwing it out of balance (like when there is jealousy in a human relationship). It's a protectiveness that is for our own good. Can you imagine if He wasn't protective of us against the attacks of the enemy? Would you feel cherished? It's the only relationship in the world where possessiveness can be equated with true, healthy love. It would feel *un*loving if God wasn't threatened by that encroachment on His turf. How special would we feel if He didn't care if the enemy had his way with us, if He was fine to let us live only a half-fulfilling life because we were too entangled in the lies? It wouldn't feel loving if He wasn't compelled to rescue us and free us. But He does feel compelled to do that—because He is jealous for us. Because we are cherished by Him.

And, oh, how He pursues us. He woos us to our most important relationship, to the moment of salvation. Then He continues to pursue us in all kinds of ways, bringing us into a deeper relationship, closer to Him and experiencing His love to a greater depth. He knows that what we really need is found when we are truly intimate with Him.

I have experienced His pursuit of me in so many ways over the time I have been with Him, I could fill a book with the stories, which, in a sense, I am doing. Times when He revealed Himself in the midst of something so that I was encouraged. Times when He taught me about my lack of something—faith, discipline, humility—so that I could grow, because He loves me too much to leave me as I am. Times when He asks things of me because He ultimately wants me to understand Him better, which benefits me tremendously and brings Him the glory He deserves at the same time.

That kind of jealousy is healthy. I welcome that kind. The kind that says "You are so important to me that I will go to the ends of the earth to show you how I feel about you and what good things I have for you." The kind of jealousy that sees me for who I am and is so passionately in love with me anyway that He goes to great lengths to make sure I know it.

He wants all of me, and He wants me to want all of Him.

Deep, Soulful Places

Listening for His Jealous Love

This past summer, I was getting ready for work when I heard a sad story on the radio. An elderly Oakville man with dementia had wandered away from his care facility and could not be found. At the time of the news bulletin, he had been missing all night. They hadn't found him the afternoon before and had searched all night to no avail, and now they were at a dead end. The prognosis was not good. Disorientation, lack of judgment and impaired decision-making would make survival overnight in the city with no food or shelter a real challenge.

What I am about to share, I am not proud of. When I heard the news bulletin, I heard God say to me, "Pray with the boys for this man—that they will find him and that he will be okay." But I shook it off. I said, *No. I'm not praying that with the boys. I don't want them to lose faith in You. The chances of this man being okay, let alone alive, at this point are pretty slim. I am not setting them up for disappointment in You by doing that.* It pains me to admit that I went back to applying my mascara.

The next time they broadcasted the story, the same thing happened. "Pray with the boys for this man—that they will find him and that he will be okay." *No. The odds are not good. I don't want to do that to them.* I began to work on my hair.

The third time the news bulletin came on, it felt very strong: "Pray with the boys for this man—that they will find him and that he will be okay." God is slow to anger, but this was one of those times. *Okay,* I said in my mind. *I will pray with them.* But I said it shaking my head, incredulous. *Why?*

I would soon find out.

I got in the car with the boys to take them to day camp. As we were driving there, I told them the story about the elderly man. I told them that we needed to pray for this man—that the police would find him and that he would be okay. Both of the boys were concerned, and one of them said, "But Mom, he might be dead."

See? Exactly what I was trying to avoid, I thought. Here was the fork in the road where I had a chance to proclaim my God and everything I claim to believe. When I got to honour our relationship and the commitment I have made to Him and He has made to me. Or not .

"Yes, he might be," I said. "But they are still looking. They haven't found him yet. And God told me we need to pray. They need our help. God asked me to pray with you that they will find him. And that when they find him, he will be okay."

So we did. In the car on the way to day camp, all three of us took turns praying for the elderly man and the search party. And when it was my turn, I found myself claiming God's power, not pleading for Him to answer. "You closed the mouths of the lions, and Daniel was not harmed. You can do this. Do the same for this man. You are God. You can help them find him, and You can keep him safe until they do. So I ask that You do that, God. That you show Your power in this situation."

I realized in that moment that God wasn't just asking me to do this for the sake of my boys and their faith. He was asking me to do it for *me*. Because He is jealous for me. Because He wants all of me. Because He wants me to passionately trust Him with every fibre, even when it doesn't make sense to my rational brain. *And* He is jealous for my kids. He wants all of them. He doesn't want me holding on to them, keeping parts of them from Him. He's too jealous for that. He wants me to surrender all of me and all of my kids to Him. And to trust Him in that. He is too jealous to let them be bound by my reaction to Him in a moment. He wants them for Himself.

I was in and out of my car quite a bit that day, and every time I would turn on the radio to hear the update. I expected to hear the good news that he had been found. By this point, I felt it was just a matter of time. God was in this. He would answer. But no luck. He hadn't been found. I found myself saying, "You can do this, God. I *know* You can."

As I was driving back to pick up the boys, the bulletin came on again. This time, the update said he had been found. Miraculously, he had managed to take the train from Oakville into downtown Toronto—a 45-minute trip. An elderly man with dementia, without his medication, food or hydration had somehow managed to safely navigate the train into downtown Toronto, and of all the places he could have wandered, they found him in one of the hospital emergency rooms. He was disoriented but completely well and unharmed, relatively emotionally unscathed by the ordeal.

As the boys climbed into the car, I told them the good news. To which they responded with a fist pump, a cheer, and a "God is so awesome!"

Yes, He is. Including His jealousy. And the fact that He wants all of us, not merely a part. Because we are cherished by Him.

The Rich Young Ruler

This morning, in my devotional time, I was directed to the story in Mark 10 of the rich young ruler who hears Jesus preaching and wants to have this eternal life Jesus is speaking about. So he asks Jesus what he needs to do. Jesus tells him he has to go and give everything he has to the poor. The Bible records that when the rich man heard this he went away sad because he had a lot of property.

Yet nestled in the story, verse 21 jumped out at me today. After the man asked Jesus what he needed to do for eternal life, verse 21 says, *"Jesus looked at him and loved him."* Jesus looked at this man with earthly success and wealth, and He knew everything. He knew that at that moment the man's wealth was his god, and that had to change because God cherishes us and is jealous for us. So Jesus did what someone who loves you does—He told the man the truth. Jesus cares about the heart. It was surrender Jesus desired.

He looked at the rich young man, straight through to his heart, and saw the war that waged within, and He loved him. Struggles and all. No condemnation, because even before salvation, there was love. This rich young ruler was seeking God. And he had found Him, in the flesh! But he wasn't yet ready to give his life over. That didn't matter to Jesus. Jesus just looked at him, and He loved him. So much.

Don't we all crave that? Someone who sees who we are, struggles and all, and nevertheless loves us? That's what Jesus does with us. We are all like the rich young ruler in some way or another. We all have things in our lives that we have put where Jesus belongs. For some of us, it may be our relationships. For others, it may be our jobs. Or maybe what we do with our free time. Maybe it's our possessions. Our accomplishments. Our children. There are many things that, if we were standing before Jesus in the flesh, He would look at us, love us and say, "First, go and take care of this." Or He would say, "You've allowed something else to fill the place where I belong."

Does any of this resonate for you? If it does, write down what God brings to your mind that He wants you to put *beneath* Him in your priority list. I know I don't ever *mean* to put something before Him, but it happens. And usually it happens subtly before I realize. The enemy, of course, doesn't want to be noticed. Jesus didn't look at the rich young ruler and rebuke him for having something in Jesus' rightful place. He didn't make the man feel two feet tall for not being up to snuff. And He didn't turn His back on the man. Jesus answered the man with truth, in love. Because Jesus *is* love.

I think it is common for females to want to experience that kind of love, the kind where someone just looks at you, and you matter to them—not because of your physical appearance but because of what you mean to them. You don't have to say a word. You don't have to prove yourself or earn their affection. They just see you, notice you, know you and love you as a result. Jesus does that for us. In fact, He does that and more. He sees right to our hearts, to all the stuff we can usually do a fairly good job of masking so that it is not visible to the human eye. And when He sees us, every single hidden part of us, He loves us. So much so, He died for us.

That makes me feel cherished. Because I *am* cherished by Him. And so are you.

"She's Mine"

Do you feel overwhelmed by His love right now? I confess, I am. How do I properly express the intensity of this? I am struck with the weight of it, wrestling with how I reflect what it means to me in a deep, soulful place. He is so jealous for you. All of you. And even knowing that all of you is not pure, right and holy. That makes me feel so safe and secure. It is almost beyond comprehension that the God of the universe is *that* passionate about *us.* That He loves us like that and is not turned off by our failings and shameful selfishness. He *cherishes* us.

He tries to tell me this all the time. He is constantly shouting from the mountaintops that I am His and that He loves me deeply. I just don't always stop and listen. And sometimes, if I'm deep enough in the valley, not paying attention, I don't even hear Him. I miss it altogether. That almost happened in the story with the lost man and my boys. I almost missed how much God cherishes me and my children—and if I had, it would have been me disoriented and lost as a result. Thankfully, just because I don't hear Him or stop to listen doesn't mean that message of love is not there. Because it is. Always. And, when I do stop and listen, when I do intentionally lift my ear up to the God of heaven, no matter how deep the valley is, His message to me is always beautiful. Always nourishing to my soul. Always one that makes me feel treasured and inexplicably whole. And sometimes, because He is so wonderful, I vicariously get blessed by witnessing His shouts of love to someone else in my life, which reminds me afresh that His passion for us knows no bounds.

A friend of mine has a strong relationship with God. She talks to Him, listens to Him, and seems to have an insatiable desire for a deeper intimacy with Him.

This past summer, in the midst of a major family issue, God revealed areas of her life that needed freedom. God called her to make some significant personal sacrifices and completely let go of *her* desires so that she could experience God in a new and beautiful way.

Now, I had been praying for my friend during this time. One day, I was getting ready for work, and God told me to send her a note. He told me to tell her that her call to personal sacrifice was for a reason. That, like Job, she was going through this so that God could demonstrate to the enemy that God did in fact have all of her and that she would "choose" God over all else in her life. Specifically, God also told me to tell her this trial was happening because God was saying to the enemy, "She's Mine. You might think these things matter, but they don't as much as *I* do. She's Mine." So I did.

Later that same day, she and her husband were praying together. Her husband asked God if He had anything He wanted to say about his wife's call to personal sacrifice. They sat in silence and listened, and God told her husband two words: "She's Mine." My friend hadn't told her husband yet about our exchange that morning. Her husband didn't know that God had told me that same message.

How awesome and beautiful is that? He loves my friend *so* much, He was so jealous for her, that His statement to her husband and the enemy was "She's *Mine*."

Oh, how God cherishes us, that He says things like that and makes sure we know it. Things that draw a clear picture of the depth and breadth of His love, that make it undeniable that He cares and doesn't leave us alone in our deep times. What a love message from Him! Through two people who didn't know the details. How clear that God was showing her just how much she is cherished by Him.

The best part, though, is that it happened a *third* time. Later on, God again prompted someone in my friend's life to tell her, "I feel like God is saying to you, 'She's Mine.' Does this fit with what God is doing in your life right now?" Um, yeah. Just a bit. Can you imagine? I'm sure it won't surprise you to hear that everything eventually worked out.

God doesn't only cherish a few of His children like this. He doesn't save these kinds of wonderful, passionate times for a select few. He loves us *all* this way. And He wants more than anything to shout to you as He shouted to my friend. You are His. *His* special possession. *His* treasure. Chosen.

Cherished.

He wants all of you and would love nothing more than to have you hear that from Him in ways that will touch those deep, soulful places in you that only He can reach.

CHAPTER NINE

The Deep, Soulful Places

I pray that you, being rooted and established in love, may have power, together with all the Lord's holy people, to grasp how wide and long and high and deep is the love of Christ.

Ephesians 3:17-18

The Prodigal Daughter

A wealthy man had two daughters. The older daughter had always done the right thing. She was obedient, responsible and everything a parent could ask for in a child. The father had never had one problem with her, and for that he was deeply thankful. He could always count on her, and his household was better for having her in it. He knew that when he was gone his eldest daughter would manage the family affairs in a way that would make him beam. He couldn't have been prouder of her if he had tried.

The man also had a younger daughter. She was the opposite of her sister. She was precocious, full of energy and curiosity. She didn't always stay within the rules intended for her own good and protection. She challenged authority as readily as medieval knights challenged one another to a duel. She was ready to leave the nest almost as soon as she got there, and everyone knew it. She was not very respectful or obedient, and it seemed she lived in a way that almost mocked the wonderful, privileged life she had been born into. Yet no one could doubt that she was still Daddy's little girl and had been from the moment she came into this world.

The wealthy father worked hard to provide not only a good life for his children, but also a good parent-child relationship. He felt that of all his wealth and possessions, it was his children who were his treasure. Oh how he loved them. And oh how it grieved his heart to watch his youngest daughter reject all he had provided. To watch her unwillingness to listen or care how her behaviour impacted others and herself was a torment he quietly bore. She began experimenting as a young girl with things he would never have dreamed any child of his would ever experiment with. Each passing day seemed to bring a greater distance between him and his little girl.

Yet despite all his patient help and pleas, one day his worst fear came true. She came and demanded that he give her all she'd get when he died. She didn't want to live under his loving rules anymore. She believed she was destined for greater things and wanted to be free. Faced with the difficult choice to either deny her request and alienate her or grant her request and let her leave with his love, he granted her request. When she left, his heart broke, and years after, people said a piece of him went with her that day. From the moment she turned her back to walk away, he longed for her return.

His little girl, out in the big, dangerous world alone, and completely unwilling to look back and see him there for her. She wanted her freedom, and she did everything to get it. At first, this newfound freedom was exhilarating, liberating, and it left her wanting more. She tried things she never even knew existed before, and for a time she wondered why she hadn't left sooner.

Eventually, however, she found herself in situations that left her feeling like a fragment of her former self. But she pushed those thoughts away and continued her downward spiral. Sometimes at a party or a club she would look back, thinking she heard her father's voice in the crowd, and she would feel a momentary surge of hope, almost relief, only to realize she was just hearing things.

Eventually this life, free as it was, started to lose its allure. As she ran out of money, she also ran out of freedom and friends. This wonderful, lavish life she felt she'd been destined for that had beckoned to her when she was at home was changing into its exact opposite. As the last of her friends and money ran out, the daughter found herself in a state of desperation. Living on the streets. Begging for food. Hiding from danger.

After a while she began risking more, exposing herself to dangerous things, maybe even in the hope of being put out of her misery. One morning, as she snuck in to wash in the public washroom of a coffee shop, a father and daughter having breakfast caught her attention. She saw her own father's loving gaze in the eyes of the stranger looking at his daughter.

There, as the grime dirtied the sink, her heart began to ache in a way she had not felt for some time. Something deep within her awoke.

She had been *loved*.

She knew it was too late, but oh, how she longed to be loved that way again. As she walked over to the table where the father and daughter had been, swiping the remains of their breakfast, she knew what she had to do.

She had thrown away the only thing that ever mattered. She knew she had no right to even set foot on her father's property, let alone ask anything of him, after how she had treated him and his money. But she also desperately wanted to believe that he would not want her living this way—especially since the servants at home lived far better than she had been living. So she resolved within herself to go home and face him. Maybe if she could just make him know how sorry she was. She couldn't expect forgiveness, but just to tell him she had been wrong. That she had taken him for granted. That she had believed the lies her friends told her about what real life was, instead of listening to the truth he told her. She decided she would ask him just one last thing, if she might be allowed to clean the stables or something. He wouldn't have to see her or what she'd become, and none of his important friends would ever have to know. She would live a quiet life as one of the help and would never breathe a word to anyone.

The more she thought about it, the more she doubted. But for the first time, she knew what was real and what wasn't—and she wanted to tell him the truth, even if he threw her out. So resigned, she started home.

Her heart was nearly beating out of her chest as she came to the corner of her father's property. Her mind was filled with fears, but her determination and strong will kept her steady on the path. Just as she stepped onto the long driveway, she noticed a figure in the distance, running towards her. At first, she was filled with fear—a guard would probably have orders from her father to send her away, knowing what she'd done, the disgrace she'd brought to him. She didn't consider the possibility of the figure being her father right away. Her father was usually in a suit and tie, on his way to or from something important – not really appropriate attire for running. But the man *was* well dressed and ran like her father, and as he was getting closer she heard a familiar voice shout, *"My little girl!"*

She turned, confused. *My little girl.* It was his special name for her.

Then she saw his face, beaming, and her fear and confusion were replaced with a sudden flood of wild hope. And she saw his eyes, lighting up in his excited face. With love! For her! It was her father running towards her. She nearly collapsed right there! Running down the path to her, his arms outstretched, he was weeping and exclaiming, "My daughter! My little girl! You're home! You're *home!*"

The daughter found her legs and began running to him too—shakily, but she couldn't help herself. He was drawing her to him. His love was palpable. She raised her arms, finally beginning to believe it. How could she have missed it all those years before, so miserable and so blind? She didn't get a chance to finish the thought, because he had reached her, swallowing her in his big arms, laughing and crying and kissing her. She hugged him back and tried to tell him she was sorry and he was right and she only wanted to ask for a job, but it was no use. He was yelling to the others who'd followed him from the house to get the celebration ready...for her. Because she came home. She tried again to say it all as he put her down and finally stood back, but he placed a finger to her lips and said, "None of that matters now. My daughter is home."

He threw her a welcome home party unlike any she'd been to before, and all his friends came even though she had left in the most disrespectful of ways. She had turned her back on him, but he would defend her and never turn his on her. Even as she ate and celebrated with him, she still couldn't believe it. She was loved—it was amazing! She was not condemned for her behaviour. She was completely forgiven. She was totally free from the life she had become enslaved to. She could let down her guard and rest because she was home. Her father was an amazing man, one whose love was unconditional and forever.

She didn't have to be afraid anymore. She was cherished, not because she deserved it, but because of who she was...

Her father's little girl.

There Is No Limit

Can you picture yourself wrapped in those arms of your Father who loves you more than you can imagine? Who sees you as you are and, regardless of everything, loves you just the same? Our heavenly Father is watching the horizon for each one of us, every day of our lives, to see when we are going to come home. To see when we will take steps towards what He wants for us.

Do you see how He watches us from His balcony, longing that we will not stray far from safety, so we can enjoy all that comes with being a child of the King? Do you see His silhouette there?

If you took His gifts and then squandered them, don't fear. Come home. He wants you there with Him. You are as wanted as the child who never left.

If you are more like the faithful older daughter who never left, His love is the same for you too. Do you see how He doesn't judge or shame? That is how He feels about you, as you muddle through trying to be the "responsible, dutiful one." And the celebration He holds for those who turn to Him—that is the joy you cause Him every day that you stay with Him and allow His love to lead you. Every day. That is how much we are loved by Him. Well, it is a glimpse of how loved we are.

When I read Ephesians 3:17–18 about His love being so wide, so long, so high and so deep for us, I am reminded yet again that there is no limit to His love. I cherish that because it means I cannot contain Him. He is not bound by me. *I* am bound by me, but He is not. Although I might limit my experience of Him because I try too hard and fail so often, that doesn't limit Him. His love is too wide, long, high and deep to be limited by anything I do or don't do.

I confess, I can be like that faithful older daughter sometimes, looking at things through this neat and tidy lens where things are fair, right and orderly. But He is not kept in that neat and tidy box, thank God. His love knows no bounds. He is as passionately in love with someone who has not been neat and tidy as He is with me. Praise God. Because I'm not really as neat and tidy as I'd like to think I am. Thankfully, God's love for me and for others does not follow what seems right to us.

And it is only as I establish myself in what He says about His love that I begin to see how wide, high, long and deep it really extends. Farther than I can see, that's for sure. Thankfully, it extends far enough that He sees me when I'm a long way off the path, coming towards Him. His love extends so far that He sees me before I even know I've been seen, and He comes running to me, genuinely missing me and wanting me close. No regard for the suit and tie, dust flying, tears streaming. That moment—when He meets me on the path, no matter how far or close I am from home, in an unconditional, loving embrace—is the most beautiful experience ever.

It makes me complete.

This is what He wants for each of His daughters. That you will know Him. That you will actually experience His love for you. Truly. That you will be rooted and established in His love for you and will be confident in it. You can have that love as the anchor in the midst of the storm. You can see Him with you in all things and understand what that means for you. He wants there to be nothing in you left unfulfilled. Because when we finally grasp how high, deep, wide and long His love for us is, it's like coming home.

Do you see Him running down the path to you with His arms stretched wide? Are you fighting His strong, gentle embrace or falling into it? Oh do it. Fall into it with reckless abandon! Relish it. Soak it in for all eternity. And as you do, you will feel Him meet you there, in those deep, soulful places that have long waited to be filled by Him.

* * *

As I wrote, seeking to share my experience of His love, I felt so loved by Him, knowing anew that there is nothing that can separate us from His love. Often as I was being obedient in sharing with you, feeling vulnerable and exposed, He met me there all over again, filling a new deep place that needed filling. It never ends with Him. He never stops meeting us where we need Him to meet us. It doesn't matter what we do, how far we stray, how hardened we are for a time; His love never fails. And He will keep pursuing us as long as we are here on this earth, because we are that important to Him. If you will decide to respond to Him, His arms will be opened so wide, ready to envelope you into an endless embrace.

At the beginning of this journey together, I shared that I was prompted to write this book because of a strong conviction that this love available to us from God is the most important thing we will ever consider in our lives. We can strip everything else away, and as long as we are left with Him and His undying love for us, we have it all. So it seems fitting to me as we walk up the driveway of our Father's mansion to the celebration inside that we pay attention to the music wafting out from the party that awaits us—music that has been playing for us all along: "Jesus loves me, this I know. For the Bible tells me so."

Appendix

Verses on God's Love

It is easy to gloss over well-known verses—they become words on a page instead of water for our souls. I have been guilty of that. These verses are just a few precious ones from many in the Bible about how loved you are by God.

Read through each verse below as though it were new to you. Look for a word you never noticed before. Find the meaning He has there for you. Drink in His love.

John 3:16   *For God so loved the world, that he gave his only Son, that whoever believes in him should not perish but have eternal life.* (ESV)

Romans 5:8   *But God shows his love for us in that while we were still sinners, Christ died for us.* (ESV)

Galatians 2:20   *I have been crucified with Christ. It is no longer I who live, but Christ who lives in me. And the life I now live in the flesh I live by faith in the Son of God, who loved me and gave himself for me.* (ESV)

1 John 4:9–11   *In this the love of God was made manifest among us, that God sent his only Son into the world, so that we might live through him. In this is love, not that we have loved God but that he loved us and sent his Son to be the propitiation for our sins. Beloved, if God so loved us, we also ought to love one another.* (ESV)

Zephaniah 3:17   *The LORD your God is in your midst, a mighty one who will save; he will rejoice over you with gladness; he will quiet you by his love; he will exult over you with loud singing.* (ESV)

Psalm 86:15   *But you, O Lord, are a God merciful and gracious, slow to anger and abounding in steadfast love and faithfulness.* (ESV)

1 John 3:1 *See what kind of love the Father has given to us, that we should be called children of God; and so we are. The reason why the world does not know us is that it did not know him.* (ESV)

Deuteronomy 7:9 *Know therefore that the LORD your God is God, the faithful God who keeps covenant and steadfast love with those who love him and keep his commandments, to a thousand generations.* (ESV)

Psalm 136:26 *Give thanks to the God of heaven, for his steadfast love endures forever.* (ESV)

In Christ...

I Am Accepted

John 1:12	I am God's child.
John 15:15	I am Christ's friend.
Romans 5:1	I have been justified.
1 Corinthians 6:17	I am united with the Lord, and I am one spirit with Him.
1 Corinthians 6:20	I have been bought with a price. I belong to God.
1 Corinthians 12:27	I am a member of Christ's Body.
Ephesians 1:1	I am a saint.
Ephesians 1:5	I have been adopted as God's child.
Ephesians 2:18	I have direct access to God through the Holy Spirit.
Colossians 1:14	I have been redeemed and forgiven of all my sins.
Colossians 2:10	I am complete in Christ.

I Am Secure

Romans 8:1,2	I am free from condemnation.
Romans 8:28	I am assured that all things work together for good.
Romans 8:31–34	I am free from any condemning charges against me.
Romans 8:35–39	I cannot be separated from the love of God.
2 Corinthians 1:21,22	I have been established, anointed and sealed by God.
Colossians 3:3	I am hidden with Christ in God.
Philippians 1:6	I am confident that the good work God has begun in me will be perfected.
Philippians 3:20	I am a citizen of heaven.
2 Timothy 1:7	I have not been given a spirit of fear, but of power, love and a sound mind.
Hebrews 4:16	I can find grace and mercy to help in time of need.
1 John 5:18	I am born of God, and the evil one cannot touch me.

I Am Significant

Matthew 5:13,14	I am the salt and light of the earth.
John 15:1,5	I am a branch of the true vine, a channel of His life.
John 15:16	I have been chosen and appointed to bear fruit.
Acts 1:8	I am a personal witness of Christ.
1 Corinthians 3:16	I am God's temple.
2 Corinthians 5:17–21	I am a minister of reconciliation for God.
2 Corinthians 6:1	I am God's co-worker (see 1 Corinthians 3:9).
Ephesians 2:6	I am seated with Christ in the heavenly realm.
Ephesians 2:10	I am God's workmanship.
Ephesians 3:12	I may approach God with freedom and confidence.
Philippians 4:13	I can do all things through Christ who strengthens me.

Neil Anderson, *Ministering the Steps to Freedom in Christ* (Eugene: Harvest House Publishers, 1998), 49.

Spiritual Warfare Readings

These resources are written by authors who have developed an expertise in this area and are offered as additional insights regarding the issue of spiritual warfare.

Neil Anderson, *Winning Spiritual Warfare* (Eugene: Harvest House Publishers, 1991).

Neil Anderson, *The Bondage Breaker,* 2nd ed. (Eugene: Harvest House Publishers, 2000).

Neil Anderson, *Victory Over Darkness* (Ventura: Regal Books, 2001).

Clinton Arnold, *3 Crucial Questions About Spiritual Warfare* (Grand Rapids: Baker Book House, 1997).

Fred Dickason, *Demon Possession and the Christian* (Chicago: Moody Press, 1987).

Charles Kraft, *I Give You Authority* (Grand Rapids: Chosen Books, 1997).

Charles Kraft, *Confronting Powerless Christianity* (Grand Rapids: Baker Book House, 2002).

Charles Kraft, *Defeating Dark Angels* (Ventura: Regal Books, 1992).

Verses About Our God

Psalm 139:1–3	*You have searched me, LORD, and you know me. You know when I sit and when I rise; you perceive my thoughts from afar. You discern my going out and my lying down; you are familiar with all my ways.*
John 14:18	*"I will not leave you as orphans; I will come to you."*
John 16:13–14	*"But when he, the Spirit of truth, comes, he will guide you into all the truth. He will not speak on his own; he will speak only what he hears, and he will tell you what is yet to come. He will glorify me because it is from me that he will receive what he will make known to you."*
Philippians 4:19	*And my God will meet all your needs according to the riches of his glory in Christ Jesus.*
2 Corinthians 3:4–5	*Such confidence we have through Christ before God. Not that we are competent in ourselves to claim anything for ourselves, but our competence comes from God.*
Hebrews 13:5–6	*God has said, "Never will I leave you; never will I forsake you." So we say with confidence, "The Lord is my helper; I will not be afraid. What can mere mortals do to me?"*
Romans 8:16–17	*The Spirit himself testifies with our spirit that we are God's children. Now if we are children, then we are heirs—heirs of God and co-heirs with Christ, if indeed we share in his sufferings in order that we may also share in his glory.*

2 Chronicles 20:17 *"You will not have to fight this battle. Take up your positions; stand firm and see the deliverance the LORD will give you, Judah and Jerusalem. Do not be afraid; do not be discouraged. Go out to face them tomorrow, and the LORD will be with you."*

Jeremiah 20:11 *But the LORD is with me like a mighty warrior; so my persecutors will stumble and not prevail. They will fail and be thoroughly disgraced; their dishonor will never be forgotten.*

1 John 4:4 *You, dear children, are from God and have overcome them, because the one who is in you is greater than the one who is in the world.*

Jeremiah 29:11 *"For I know the plans I have for you," declares the LORD, "plans to prosper you and not to harm you, plans to give you hope and a future."*

Psalm 138:7–8 *Though I walk in the midst of trouble, you preserve my life. You stretch out your hand against the anger of my foes; with your right hand you save me. The LORD will vindicate me; your love, LORD, endures forever—do not abandon the works of your hands.*

Isaiah 41:10 *So do not fear, for I am with you; do not be dismayed, for I am your God. I will strengthen you and help you; I will uphold you with my righteous right hand.*

Isaiah 55:6–9 *Seek the LORD while he may be found; call on him while he is near. Let the wicked forsake their ways and the unrighteous their thoughts. Let them turn to the LORD, and he will have mercy on them, and to our God, for he will freely pardon. "For my thoughts are not your thoughts, neither are your ways my ways," declares the LORD. "As the heavens are higher than the earth, so are my ways higher than your ways and my thoughts than your thoughts."*

Thoughts About Salvation and Forgiveness

I wanted to share my thoughts on salvation for those who may not be sure what I am talking about when I refer to salvation and Jesus' sacrifice for us on the cross. Before I explain, however, I'd like to reiterate one fundamental truth to frame this discussion: *God is love.* His desires for us, His response to us, His willingness to give us free will and His sacrifice for us all come from that unending, all-encompassing love. So, quiet all the noise of your past, all the negative, punitive things that may have muddied the waters for you concerning this truth, and consider salvation as a love offering. Completely and fully. For you.

Salvation

God created this world to be perfect. He made it with the same care, attention and passion as an artist creates a masterpiece. It was untainted and as lavish and pure as could be. It was His desire that humankind live in perfect harmony with Him forever—unhindered by pain, hardship and sin. But He also made us with free will so that we could choose Him, rather than having no choice. Love is so much richer and more beautiful when it flows from within rather than being prescribed from without.

The enemy of our souls interfered and offered humankind a choice against God. Satan did not like that God was receiving all this love and attention and wanted to do something to ruin God's plans. Adam and Eve accepted the offer.

Because of Adam and Eve's sin in the Garden of Eden, the perfect fellowship they had with God was broken, and something was needed to restore it. Why would God bother to do this for us? Jeremiah 31:3 says, *"I have loved you with an everlasting love."* His love for us will never change. The Bible records years of God setting in motion and ultimately revealing His plan to offer a second chance to humankind out of His deep and unending love for us. John 3:16 says, *"For God so loved the world that he gave his one and only Son, that whoever believes in him shall not perish but have eternal life."*

Deep, Soulful Places

The Bible says if you believe in Jesus and "confess your sins" (which means to own up to the fact that compared to God, you fall short, you do things wrong that go against His character, you are not perfect, and you can't maintain a level of goodness that makes you "suitable" in and of yourself for heaven), He will forgive you and cleanse you.

Adam and Eve sinned and broke the perfect relationship with God, but there is a second chance. We don't have to remain destined to a life without God. Jesus Christ died on the cross and rose again to pay the price that needed to be paid. That sacrifice gives us inherent worth far above anything this world could ever offer. And He did it for you and for me. We are *so* loved that we are offered freedom! And this sacrifice speaks powerfully to our worth because of the price that was paid to keep us. No wonder it is often referred to as the Good News!

Confession and Forgiveness

Salvation comes from accepting what Jesus did for us on the cross. At that point, our sins are no longer held against us, and we are made right with God. Which means that one day, when we die, we will spend eternity in heaven with Him. And that is secure. Once, for all, the Bible says.

However, just like your marriage relationship needs to be nurtured and cared for after you commit to your marriage partner in a ceremony and seal the deal, so our relationship with God needs to be maintained. When I do something dumb (which is unfortunately way more often than I care to admit) and upset my husband, I apologize to him. Why? Not because I need to in order to keep us married. Not because he will stop loving me if I don't. I apologize because it keeps our relationship on the right track. It keeps nothing between us, so that our love and intimacy can grow. You do the same with friends, neighbours and coworkers when it is a relationship that you want to stay strong and good, right?

The same dynamic exists in our relationship with Christ. Making mistakes and sinning after we are saved doesn't stop or end our salvation. That's not why we confess those sins and ask forgiveness. We do it because it keeps the lines of communication open with God. It allows us to do our part in making sure that nothing gets in the way of that relationship, so that we can grow in our love and intimacy with Him.

It is not about ensuring we stay loved or saved. It's about ensuring we stay as open and close as we can, so we can receive as fully as possible all He has waiting for us in our relationship with Him.

Thoughts About Abuse

Abuse was discussed in the chapter titled "No Fear" because I couldn't talk about fear without acknowledging one of the most prevalent causes of it. But it really deserves more than a mention, due to the extent to which we see it around us and the immense damage it does in our lives.

Physical, emotional, psychological, sexual and verbal abuse teaches lies. There is nothing right, lovely, pure or good about abuse. Abuse teaches lies such as "I need to fear authority or rebel against it," "Anger is bad, scary or painful," "I don't deserve to be safe," "Making mistakes hurts," "I need to be perfect," "I should hate myself," "No one loves me," "When I hurt others I can have power," "If you are bigger, you can hurt others," and "My feelings don't matter." And the list goes on. If God is love, anything that evokes the pain and distortion in these lies is not sanctioned by God and is not love. It is therefore not okay. Ever.

The enemy would love us to believe that there are times when abuse is okay. Or times when it is supported by God. Many abuse victims talk about times when they cried out to God for help and the abuse still happened, so they figured either it must have been okay with God or He didn't care enough to save them. Those are lies. You are worth saving. He does care.

I can't speak to why things unfolded for you the way they did in your particular situation. I'm sorry it happened. It shouldn't have. You didn't deserve it, and it was wrong. But hear me: abuse is not evidence of a lack of God's love. You have every right to feel hurt, confused and a whole host of other feelings about it, but don't let the enemy make an already rotten, unfair situation worse by tricking you into believing lies about yourself and the God who loves you.

Find someone you trust who can talk about these things with you. Your pain and your experience deserve attention, care and healing. And talk with God about it. He will answer you. He is not who the enemy says He is.

He is *Love*.

Deep, Soulful Places

Intimate Partner Abuse

Despite all the education, advocacy and awareness, abuse is reaching mammoth proportions these days. And it is often justified through the misuse of the Bible. It is domestic violence, the use of power and control in an intimate relationship. And it is wrong. It is not pleasing to God. If this is happening to you, it is not your fault. Ever.

This might not be something you have any personal experience with. But read on, because it is happening to someone you know. The statistics are staggering. Where I live, police report responding to an average of 13 domestic violence calls *per day,* and 3 out of 4 women experience it at some point in their lives. Sadly, a woman is murdered every 6 days in Canada because of this issue. The two most commonly misquoted passages used to justify abuse are Colossians 3:18, *"Wives, submit yourselves to your husbands, as is fitting in the Lord,"* and Ephesians 5:22–24,

> *Wives, submit yourselves to your own husbands as you do to the Lord. For the husband is the head of the wife as Christ is the head of the church, his body, of which he is the Savior. Now as the church submits to Christ, so also wives should submit to their husbands in everything.*

Those verses form the "scriptural" foundation for violence: "You were not submitting." "It is my right as the head of the home." "God says."

Interestingly, other verses that provide context are somehow left out: *"Husbands, **love** your wives and **do not be harsh** with them"* (Colossians 3:19, emphasis added). This leaves no basis for husbands to think it is okay to abuse or demean their wives. Then in Ephesians 5:25, 28–29,

> *Husbands, love your wives, just as Christ loved the church and gave himself up for her...In this same way, husbands ought to love their wives as their own bodies. He who loves his wife loves himself. After all, no one ever hated their own body, but they feed and care for their body, just as Christ does the church.*

Christ loved the Church, served it and then gave His life for it. That does not sound abusive or harsh. That sounds immensely loving and self-sacrificial, and that is what husbands are called to. Anything else is not sanctioned by God, and you do not have to suffer it in the name of submission.

In fact, God gave us a blueprint for beautiful relationships as He designed them. We are to show each other self-sacrificial love like Jesus showed us (John 15:12) and mutual submission and respect because of Christ (Ephesians 5:21, 33). And when He is our motivation (not selfishness, power, control or neediness), when we love each other deeply, we are told in 1 Peter 4:8, *"Love covers over a multitude of sins."*

Love doesn't expose sins and make people feel shame, ridicule and embarrassment for them; it covers over them. Godly, pure, biblical love doesn't focus on self; it strives to serve, sacrifice and give—like Christ did for us. Never once will you find a verse that talks about how Jesus' love for someone resulted in Him hurting them or making them feel like they were worthless. Jesus' love never dominated or controlled. Jesus' love never made someone afraid for her life. Jesus' love never made someone flee so she would no longer be beaten.

If you are being abused or know of a child who is being abused, tell someone who can help. You are not alone. There is help.

If you are in Canada, calling either of these numbers will put you in touch with someone who can help you connect with the right services:

Assaulted Women's Helpline:
1–866–863–0511 (www.awhl.org)

Kids Help Phone:
1–800–668–6868 (www.kidshelpphone.ca)

Family Service Canada

For a counselling agency in your area, visit www.familyservicecanada.org and under "Membership info" click on "Current Members (by province)" It will list counselling centres by province. If you don't see one close enough to you, call the one that is the closest and ask for their help.

Regardless of what country you are in, if you search "counselling for abuse" along with your city or town, you will be given a list of agencies in your area that you can reach out to.

Appendix G

Recommended Readings

Buchanan, Mark. *The Rest of God: Restoring your Soul by Restoring Sabbath.* Nashville: Thomas Nelson, 2006.

Eldridge, Stasi. *Captivating: Unveiling the Mystery of a Woman's Soul.* Nashville: Thomas Nelson, 2005.

Lin, Merry C. *The Fully Lived Life: Rescuing Our Souls from All that Holds us Back.* Pickering: Castle Quay Books, 2014.

Moore, Beth. *Get out of that Pit: Straight Talk about God's Deliverance.* Nashville: Thomas Nelson, 2007.

Shrirer, Priscilla. *A Jewel in His Crown.* Chicago: Moody Press, 1999.

Yancy, Phillip. *What's so Amazing about Grace?* Grand Rapids: Zondervan, 1997.

Acknowledgements

Of the whole book, I think this might have been the hardest page to write. Not because I don't know who to thank, but because I don't know where to begin.

Without a publisher and publishing editor, there would be no book, so thank you to Larry and Marina Willard of Castle Quay Books for making this book become something more than a file on my computer. Your guidance, wisdom, personal care, attention to detail and professionalism are more than I could have hoped for in this process. May God richly bless you and the ministry you have for Him.

And then there is Mick Silva. So much more than "just" an editor/coach. Throughout the process you were someone who encouraged me, believed in me and challenged me to be better. And most importantly, you were invested in listening to the Holy Spirit and ensuring that everything that was done fell in line with His leading. Doesn't get much better than that. You were an answer to prayer for me, and I know you will be the same for many others.

I also had a group of friends who surrounded me with their prayer, love and encouragement. Deb and Jamie, Morgan, Merry, Sarah and Graham, Joscelyn, Angela, Monica, Beth, Greg and Heather. Thanks for your faithful prayers, for listening to me as I talked incessantly about the book and for not letting me get distracted from my goal. A special mention has to go to Deb, who has walked this journey with me from before I wrote the first word. You have been a relentless source of immense support to me, to my face and in the quiet time you spent with Him on my behalf. Thank you.

My family has also offered me invaluable encouragement and prayer support—both sets of parents, siblings and siblings-in-law. I'm so thankful to have family who are willing to stand in the gap for me in the most meaningful way. Not that I'm surprised; that's just who you all are.

Thanks to my friends at YWG! You encouraged me, critiqued me and helped me write better. I learned so much from you, and I so value your support and prayers! A higher purpose really is the best.

And last, but certainly not least, I owe enormous gratitude to my husband, Todd, and my boys, Ethan and Caleb. Without your complete and unselfish support of me, I would not have been able to do this. Todd, you are the reason I started this book to begin with. Well, I guess technically it was the Holy Spirit through your wise encouragement. You have been a steady force, an unwavering cheerleader and an unflappable sounding board. You are my best friend, my safest earthly place, and I love you more than I know how to express.

My boys have tolerated many an hour with my back to them as I sat at the computer. They have also both been faithful in praying for me and have given me their pearls of wisdom along the way, which have been deeply encouraging. Thank you, Ethan, for those bedtime chats when you would share your heart with me and encourage me to do this. Thanks for calling me an "author" before I ever considered myself to be one. Thank you, Caleb, for the sincere interest you showed in what I was writing through the questions you asked and for always remembering to pray for me. I love you both so much.

I think it's fitting to end by quoting Caleb's prayer that he has literally prayed every night since I began writing: "God, please help my mother's book [get finished/get published], so that people can read her book. And I pray that lots of people will read her book, and when they read her book that they will love you and give their 100 percent trust to you, and then they will tell other people to read her book and they will give their trust to you, and so on." Amen, Caleb. Amen.

About the Author

Elizabeth Pierce is a wife, mother of two, and clinical social worker by profession. She never intended to be an author. Her goal was simple—to "make a difference" in this world. She always thought that meant one person at a time in a counselling session. However, when God began asking her to do things that didn't fit inside the four safe walls of an office, she became aware that she was being led on a journey to fulfill the plan *God* had in store for her. *Deep, Soulful Places* is a culmination of all that transpired, personally and professionally, as she sought to be a vessel for Him. When she is not at work, she lives a busy life, full of children's sporting events, serving in her church and spending time with the important people God has blessed her with. Most importantly, though, she is tenderly yet passionately pursued every day by a loving God and wants to ensure that everyone else understands that they are too.

.

CPSIA information can be obtained at www.ICGtesting.com
Printed in the USA
LVOW04s0436141015

458198LV00036B/645/P